Truth Encounter

A Bible Study for Catholics

Dr. Anthony Pezzotta
with Terry Dalrymple

TRUTH ENCOUNTER
Copyright © 1996 Anthony Pezzotta

Published by
Foreign Mission Board, SBC

No part of this book may be reproduced
in any manner without the written permission
of the publisher.

Requests for information should be addressed to
CHURCH STRENGTHENING MINISTRY
P.O. Box 2656 MCPO, 1266 Makati City

ISBN 971-717-040-1

Unless otherwise indicated, biblical quotations
are from: The Holy Bible, *New International Version,*
Copyright © 1973, 1978, 1984 by International Bible Society.
Used by permission.

First printed February 1996

10 9 8 7 6

Cover Design by: Benjamin Fallorina, Jr. and Leo Moralina

Printed in the Republic of the Philippines.

To God Alone
Be All The Glory

DEDICATION

Lovingly dedicated to my wife, ZITA, whose faithful love and support has helped keep me going, and whose simple but strong faith has been a constant inspiration.

ACKNOWLEDGMENT

I want to express sincere gratitude:

To my mission, CB International, Philippines, for giving me encouragement, support and time to write this book.

To my colleague Cheri Strahm for careful editing.

To Rev. Claude King for meaningful contributions and heartfelt support.

Table of Contents

Foreword

*T*he release last year of "Evangelicals and Catholics Together: The Christian Mission in the Third Millennium," reopened the dormant and divisive tension between Evangelicals and Catholics. The recent publications of "House United: Evangelicals and Catholics Together" by Keith A. Fournier with William D. Watkins (Colorado: NavPress Publishing Group, 1994) and "Roman Catholicism: Evangelical Protestants Analyze What Divides and Unites Us" by John Armstrong, General Editor, (Chicago: Moody Press, 1994) were indicative of the renewed debate.

There is a growing consensus to form an "ecumenism on the trenches" among Evangelicals, Catholics and other groups to combine their arsenals in a common culture war against repression of religious liberty, abortions, pornography, antireligious bigotry in media, the celebration of violence, and all forms of immoralities. This is grounded on justice and common grace. We uphold the dignity of man and woman as created in the image of God and respect their free will to worship or not to worship Him.

The conflict is on ecumenism in evangelism and mission. There are two basic issues to be resolved: (1) The use of common language. There is a lot of common language used by Catholics and Evangelicals such as the Gospel, Justification

i

by Faith, and Evangelism. The question is: Is there a common meaning to the words used? For example, is there a common understanding of the *evangel* or the Gospel? Are there changes in Roman Catholic doctrines since the Council of Trent or the Vatican Council II? This "cloud of unknowing" is part of the critical problem in Evangelical-Catholic relationship. (2) The meaning of affirmations. There are affirmations being done on doctrines but there are no rejections of corollary ones. For example, when a person says that the Holy Bible is authoritative does he also deny the equal authority of Tradition or the Papacy? Or when he says that salvation is only through faith in Jesus Christ, does he deny the validity of baptism or church membership as a means of entrance into heaven?

The Agreement says: "The achievement of good will and cooperation between Evangelicals and Catholics must not be at the price of the urgency and clarity of Christian witness to the Gospel." Clearly, it is a warning not to dilute grave, even irreconcilable, doctrinal differences. The doctrines and practices must be reviewed for reaffirmation or rejection. There is a danger in using the word Evangelical simply as an adjective and not as a noun. As an *adjective*, one can redefine the meaning of the word to suit his personal preferences or understanding. One can change the language used in the mass, but has there been a change in the doctrinal meaning of the eucharist in the Catholic church? As a *noun*, it has a normative weight in that includes its history, its institutions, its Truth-claims and practices. There can be no unity of religion and plurality of truth. Because one's religious faith is a life and death issue, it is necessary that Truth-claims must be examined.

Rev. Pezzotta cited a quote from Cardinal Sin on the occasion of the death of Pope Paul VI in 1978: "Dearly beloved . . . Although we *hope* that by now he is enjoying that eternal life which he strove so hard to merit, nevertheless, not knowing the inscrutable plan of Almighty God, let us pray for his soul, that it may soon reach the well deserved bliss." This is the heart of the problem. Is there an objective Truth upon which one's eternal destiny is to depend rather than the frailty of sinful man? The Apostle John wrote in no uncertain terms, "that you may know that you have eternal life" (1 Jn. 5:13). Religious faith is not a matter of taste but of Truth. A person can change religion anytime but Truth is unchanging.

The book, *Truth Encounter*, by Rev. Anthony Pezzotta comes to us fresh today. It is a spiritual journey of a former Catholic priest, scholar, and a theologian. It is a powerful story of his painful search for Truth in the Holy Bible. It is an inspiring testimony of his conversion—the renewing of his mind, the forgiveness of his sins, the reality of life eternal in Christ. As a man of God and of the Word, his life and lifestyle in his ministry and family have demonstrated consistent evidences of Christian authenticity and God's transforming grace.

In his book, he follows a format: doctrines, history, practices, and Scripture. He examines, as one who knew Catholicism from within, a wide range of fundamental Catholic beliefs and practices and scrutinizes them in the light of God's Word. He has the intellectual credential, experiential credibility, and moral authority to do so. Like His Lord, Rev. Pezzotta is pleading, *"let's reason together"* (Isa. 1:18). *Truth Encounter* is a thought-provoking workbook that challenges one's beliefs to its very roots. As one reads through the book, he will find that the encounter is not with the author but with Jesus Christ, *"the way, the truth, and the life . . ."* (Jn. 14:6).

This book, however, is not to be used as a club but as an offer of love. There are wheats to nurture among the Catholics and weeds to evangelize among the Protestants. Evangelicals must build relationship of cordiality with Catholics and other religious groups but cordiality is not to lead to confusion and compromise of Truth. God's Word should be the sole arbiter of truth in evaluating the doctrines and deeds of Catholics, Protestants, and groups. Therefore, the book is to be used with prayers and tears especially for those who have zeal of God but not according to knowledge. Truth can hurt but as Jesus Christ says, *"The truth shall set you free"* (Jn. 8:32). Salvation is in the works of Christ (at the cross) not in the works of man. Saving faith, informed in the mind by the Word of Truth, created in the heart by the active work of the Holy Spirit, should produce fruits of repentance, good works, and outside service of God to man. Upon these foundations can one find life eternal and a transcendent purpose to serve God for His glory.

Dr. Agustin B. Vencer, Jr.
International Director
World Evangelical Fellowship

Introduction

An Encounter with God is an Encounter with Truth

Yahweh is the *God of Truth* (Isaiah 65:16).
Jesus is the Way and *the Truth* (John 14:6).
The Holy Spirit is the *Spirit of Truth* (John 16:13).
The Word of God is the *Word of Truth*
    (2 Timothy 2:15).

We cannot encounter the God of Christianity without encountering truth. Jesus said to his disciples: *"You will know the truth, and the truth will set you free."*

Truth is Needed for Genuine Conversion

Conversion to Christ involves *repentance* and *faith*. Both are activities of the mind and will *in response to truth*.

1

The New Testament word for *repentance* means literally *a change of mind*.[1] This involves two acknowledgments:

(1) that our ways are wrong and evil

(2) that God's ways are right

God's ways (Truth) are revealed in the Holy Scriptures. We repent by understanding the truth of God's Word and changing our thinking so that we choose to act in a way that is consistent with God's purposes.

Repentance is an activity of the mind and will. Our emotions and heart are involved, but more as a result of our decision than as the root of it! Jesus, John the Baptist, and Peter viewed repentance in this way (Matthew 4:17; Matthew 3:2; Acts 2:38).

Likewise, the New Testament word for *faith* [2] refers to an activity of the mind and will, *in response to truth*. The word "faith" in Greek derives from a root word which means *to be inwardly convinced, persuaded*.[3] Biblical faith begins in the mind *with knowledge of the truth* and works itself out through the will when one personally trusts Christ for forgiveness of sins and the gift of eternal life. Biblical faith is both belief in the truth and trust in the Savior.

Genuine conversion is based on knowledge of the TRUTH about ourselves and about God. We must *understand* that we are hopeless and helpless sinners, and that God loves us and will save through

Repentance and faith are activities of the mind and will in response to TRUTH.

JESUS all those who repent and believe and trust in Him.

---

[1]*Μετανοια, οιας, η, (Μετανοεω)*: "A change of mind: as it appears in one who repents of a purpose he has formed or of something he has done . . ." (*Thayer's Greek-English Lexicon of the New Testament*, Zondervan Publishing House, Grand Rapids, 1974, p. 405).

[2]*Πιστις, εως, η, (πειθω)*: "Conviction of the truth of anything, belief . . . generally with the included idea of trust . . ." (Ibid., p. 512).

[3]*Πειθω* is the root word from which the word *πιστις* is derived. *Πειθω* means 1. "To persuade." 2. "To be persuaded" (Middle). 3. "To trust, have confidence." (Ibid., p. 497).

Truth is Necessary for Christian Living

Knowledge of the truth should determine how we live, and help us to live above our negative feelings and emotions:

> Love over fear,
>> Obedience over rebellion,
>>> Trust over despair,
>>>> Humility over pride.

Truth, not feelings, should guide us in our spiritual walk (2 John 4; Galatians 2:11).

Truth is a Reliable Guide, Emotion is Not

Many new "believers" seem to easily give up their faith because their relationship relies more on emotion than on an encounter with the truth (Matthew 13:20, 21). Genuine conversion is not the result of an emotional need being met nor the reaction to a supernatural event strongly affecting emotion, but a real encounter with the revealed truth about oneself, God and Christ Jesus.

No one feels like turning the other cheek. Love does it anyway! God expects the Christian to walk in love. This love in which we walk is not based on emotion and feeling. When we do love God and neighbor wholeheartedly, our emotions and feelings are affected. However, what we feel is the fruit of love, not the root of it. Genuine love is a result of faith and is expressed *in obedience to the truth*, faithfulness, self-control, kindness, and goodness.[4]

---

[4]"Now that you have purified yourselves by obeying the truth, so that you have sincere love for your brothers, love one another deeply, from the heart" (1 Peter 1:22).

◆   Read attentively the following statement from the Lord Jesus. Mark the statements below that are *true* with a "T." Mark those statements that are inconsistent with the teaching of Jesus with an "F" for *false*.

> [20]*The one who received the seed that fell on rocky places is the man who hears the word and at once receives it with joy.* [21]*But since he has no root, he lasts only a short time. When trouble or persecution comes because of the word, he quickly falls away (Matthew 13:20, 21).*

_____ Joyful experiences always produce lasting faith.

_____ Joy gives a believer roots that will support him in his walk with God through all kinds of hardship and persecution.

_____ Faith is much more than feelings of joy. Lasting faith is grounded in convictions (truth) that do not change with time or circumstance.

Truth is a Reliable Guide, Experience Not Always

I decided to entitle this book <u>Truth Encounter</u> not to deny the reality of the "power encounter," but to emphasize the importance of truth. Not everyone needs a power encounter, but everyone does need an encounter with truth. The encounter with truth is basic and is far more important than the power encounter in both our conversion experience and our daily walk with the Lord.

Truth is a more reliable guide than emotion or experience in matters of faith and practice.

God clearly teaches that the criterion for believing and following a preacher, teacher, or prophet, is not the miracles he performs but the substance of his teaching, even if the miracles are true.

¹If a prophet, or one who foretells by dreams, appears among you and announces to you a miraculous sign or wonder, ²and if the sign or wonder of which he has spoken takes place, and he says, "Let us follow other gods" (gods you have never known), "and let us worship them," ³you must not listen to the words of that prophet or dreamer (Deuteronomy 13:1-3).

♦ Read attentively the following statement from the Lord Jesus. Mark the statements below that are *true* with a "T". Mark those statements that are inconsistent with the teaching of Jesus with an "F" for *false*.

²²Many will say to me on that day, "Lord, Lord, did we not prophesy in your name, and in your name drive out demons and perform many miracles?" ²³This I will tell them plainly, "I never knew you. Away from me, you evildoers!" ²⁴Therefore everyone who hears these words of mine and puts them into practice is like a wise man who built his house on the rock (Matthew 7:22-24).

_____ A miracle is proof that God is speaking through a particular person.

_____ Evildoers who do not know the Lord can do miracles "in His name."

_____ The Words of Jesus, not miracles or prophecies, should be the foundation of our belief and behavior.

♦ Read attentively the following statement from the apostle Paul. Mark the statements below that are *true* with a "T". Mark those statements that are inconsistent with the teaching of Jesus with an "F" for *false*.

But even if we, or an angel from heaven, should preach a gospel other than the one we preached, let him be eternally condemned (Galatians 1:8).

_____ People should always maintain allegiance to the teachings of angels or other spiritual persons who appear to the faithful.

_____ People should maintain allegiance to the teachings of one who appears only if his/her message is consistent with the teachings of the Gospel proclaimed by Christ himself and His apostles after him.

_____ Any teaching that is contrary to the message of the Gospel as recorded by Christ's own apostles in the Holy Scriptures must be rejected, even if someone should appear "from heaven" to proclaim it.

Truth is the Basis of Christian Unity

Truth is foundational and essential, and believers are not allowed to compromise with clearly revealed truth for any reason, even for the sake of love and unity. Without truth people might be united in error. What good would that bring?

A patient once went to the doctor with "pain in his chest." The doctor quickly diagnosed the pains as angina. He shared his conclusions with several of his peers who joined him in recommending that the patient have open heart surgery. The doctors stood united in their decision. There was harmony. They spoke with one voice. They had a wonderful working relationship.

The patient decided to get one more opinion from a doctor not connected with the first. This second doctor revealed that he did not have heart problems at all. He had heartburn. A few antacids, and the "angina" disappeared!

The first doctors were united. The second one had the truth! We must never compromise truth for the sake of unity.

Conclusion

By experience I know that many Roman Catholics are sincere in their beliefs and are looking for the truth. This book therefore is

Clearly revealed truth from God's Word is the only fully reliable guide on our spiritual journey.

intended to assist them in finding the truth of God's Word. It is also meant to help evangelical Christians have a more objective understanding of Catholicism and enable them to share more effectively, "speaking the truth in love" (Ephesians 4:15).

◆ Check those statements which have been true of your religious experience.

_____ I'm not that concerned with the truth. Nobody can know for sure what it is.

_____ I do not allow myself to think about whether or not my church teaches the truth. I am loyal and committed to my church regardless.

_____ My religious experience has been one long search for the truth.

_____ I will not belong to a church that does not teach the truth.

◆ Write a prayer in the space provided below, asking God to help you know Him better and to guide you into a deeper encounter with the truth.

_____

_____

_____.

Chapter 1

The Word Of Truth

*T*hree years before I became a priest, I picked up an Anglican catechism and read the commandments of God. I read the fifth commandment. It said, "Honor your father and your mother." I thought, "No, that is the fourth." In my ingenuity and pride, being a Catholic, I said, "Look at these blessed Anglicans. They don't even know the ten commandments of God!" Then I saw that the second commandment was something new to me. I went to the Bible and found out that their catechism was right!

In all Catholic catechisms and theology books, this fifth commandment to honor your father and mother is the fourth. They took away the second commandment which says: [4]*"You shall not make yourself a carved image or any likeness of anything in heaven or on earth beneath or in the waters under the earth;* [5]*you shall not bow down to them or serve them. For I, Yahweh your God, am a jealous God . . ."* (Exodus 20:4, 5, Jerusalem Bible). In order to come up with ten, they divided the last commandment, which in the Bible is one, into two commands.

Who Has the Truth?

The world is full of religious messengers and messages. Some are teaching the truth. Some are teaching error. There are more than 5 billion people in the world, 1.5 billion of them claiming to be Christian. They are very sincere in their beliefs and practices. However, they cannot ALL be right. Most are sincere, but some are sincerely wrong (Romans 10:1, 2).

This fact should cause the honest person to ask WHY he believes what he believes. Every religious thought has its source. There is a person, an AUTHORITY or a teacher, behind every belief held by men. Whether consciously or unconsciously, men who believe have chosen to put their trust in a person. The real question is "Who?"

The Truth is in Jesus

There is ONE unique person in history who we all agree should be trusted. He calmed storms with a word, walked on water, made water wine, cast out demons, caused the lame to walk, caused the blind to see, and even raised the dead. He predicted His own death at the hands of the chief priests and promised to rise again. He rose from the dead, as He promised He would, and showed Himself to more than 500 witnesses. He gave authority to His disciples to do miracles, and in His name they healed the sick, cast out demons, and raised the dead. His teachings, right and true, changed the course of human history. Indeed He was, as He claimed to be, the Son of God. THIS ONE IS JESUS CHRIST.

We are called "Christian" because we are followers of Christ. He is THE TEACHER we choose to believe. His teachings are found in the BIBLE. The Bible is divided into two parts: The Old Testament and the New Testament.

Jesus Taught that the Truth is in the Scriptures

The Old Testament was written before Jesus lived. The New Testament was written after His resurrection. Jesus taught His followers that the Old Testament Scriptures are the Word of God. He upheld the Old Testament Scriptures as infallible, and regarded them to be the FINAL AUTHORITY for faith and practice (Matthew 5:17-20).

The New Testament is a written record of the teachings of Jesus Himself, and His appointed messengers. While Jesus was here on earth, He chose apostles (messengers) to deliver His message to the world. These men learned at the feet of Jesus and are eye-witnesses to the miracles He performed, to His death, and to His resurrection. The teachings of the Christian Church are based upon the message of these apostles or disciples. We read in Acts that the early Church devoted itself to the *"apostles' teaching"* (Acts 2:42), and in Ephesians that the Church was *"built on the foundation of the apostles and prophets, with Christ Jesus Himself as the chief cornerstone"* (Ephesians 2:20). We have a written record of their teachings, which originated with Jesus, in the New Testament.

The teachings of Jesus are recorded in the Bible.

Until today, every Christian group recognizes the Bible as a sacred book. Here is what the Catholic Church teaches:

> *Holy Scripture comprises the sacred books of the Old and New Testaments. These, with all their parts, are INSPIRED by God and HAVE HIM for AUTHOR, and are therefore FREE FROM ERROR, not only in moral and religious statements (The Teaching of the Catholic Church, by Roos and Neuner, Jesuits; ed. Karl Rahner, Jesuit).*

Three Contemporary Answers to the Question: "Who has the Truth?"

While every Christian group recognizes the Bible as sacred, not all view the Bible as the FINAL AUTHORITY in matters of faith and practice. All Christian churches fall into one of three categories:

1. Those who believe that church leaders (Bishops, Popes) have final authority
2. Those who believe that reason is the final authority
3. Those who believe that God's written Word (The Bible) is the final authority

The conservative members of institutional churches (Catholic, Greek Orthodox, and others) belong to the first group. They honor the Bible, but hold onto traditions. Their final authority is their church leaders. For these, the truth is what their church teaches.

The liberal members of various churches belong to the second group. They have a certain respect for the Bible, for traditions, and for religious leaders; yet, they believe and do only what seems acceptable to their own way of thinking. They themselves are their own final authority. For this group of people, the truth is what their reason supports.

Evangelical Christians and all those who are "born again" constitute the third group. They respect and accept traditions and the teaching of religious leaders only when those traditions and teachings are in keeping with God's written Word. The Bible is their supreme and final authority. For these, the truth is what is recorded in the Bible.

Jesus' answer to the Question: "Where is the truth?"

On the question of authority, Jesus spoke very clearly. In Matthew chapter fifteen, Jesus upholds the written Scriptures as the supreme and final authority in matters of faith and practice. He taught His disciples to reject any teaching that is contrary to the written Word of God.

> [1]*Then some Pharisees and teachers of the law came to Jesus from Jerusalem and asked,* [2]*"Why do your disciples break the tradition of the elders? They don't wash their hands before they eat!"*
>
> [3]*Jesus replied, "And why do you break the command of God for the sake of your tradition?* [4]*For God said, 'Honor your father and mother' and 'Anyone who curses his father or mother must be put to death.'* [5]*But you say that if a man says to his father or mother, 'Whatever help you might otherwise have received from me is a gift devoted to God,'* [6]*he is not to 'honor his father' with it. Thus you nullify the Word of God for the sake of your tradition.* [7]*You hypocrites! Isaiah was right when he prophesied about you:* [8]*'These people honor me with their lips, but their hearts are far from me.* [9]*They worship me in vain; their teachings are but rules taught by men' "* (Matthew 15:1-9).

The Setting, Matthew 15:1

Certain religious leaders approached Jesus, accusing His disciples of breaking one of their religious traditions. In this passage, Jesus Himself speaks concerning the role of tradition and the authority of the Scriptures.

The Religious Leaders, Matthew 15:1

The Pharisees were religious leaders and also a nationalistic political party. As a political party, they opposed colonization by Rome and resisted the colonizers themselves. As religious leaders, they studied and interpreted the Word of God for the people.

The Religious Traditions, Matthew 15:2

The religious traditions mentioned here are found in the Talmud. They are interpretations and additions that the Pharisees and the scribes made to the Word of God and to the ceremonial laws of the Old Testament.

The Accusation, Matthew 15:2

The Pharisees taught that washing before eating made one acceptable to God. Those who did not wash their hands before eating were sinning—they became impure in their souls. Their tradition instructed the people always to wash their hands before eating.

Jesus and His disciples washed their hands when it was convenient. Their failure to comply with this religious ritual aggravated the Pharisees. They asked Jesus: "Why do your disciples break the tradition of the elders? They don't wash their hands before they eat!"

The Defense, Matthew 15:3-9

Jesus answered the Pharisees with an accusation of His own: "Why do you break the commandment of God for the sake of your tradition?" He substantiated His accusation with an example to show that He was talking the truth. He quoted the fifth commandment from the law of Moses in Exodus 20: "For God said, Honor your father and mother, and anyone who curses father or mother must be put to death."

The word "honor," in both Hebrew and Greek, carries with it the idea of financial support. To honor a parent is to support him or her financially. Children should see to it that their parents have the same standard of living that they have attained. The English word "honorarium" derives from this idea. Those who rise into the upper class while leaving their parents to live as squatters violate this command of love and respect. Jesus understands "honor" to include financial support.

When it comes to the Word of God, what God forbids or commands in the Scriptures, Jesus has the highest respect. He presents Himself as one who came

Final authority rests with the written Scriptures, not the religious leaders or the traditions.

to fulfill the Old Testament Scriptures (Matthew 5:17-20). Jesus was not concerned that His disciples failed to comply with tradition, but He was very concerned that the Pharisees failed to comply with the commands of Scripture.

After quoting the fifth commandment, Jesus quoted from the Talmud in order to identify the error that was being practiced.

> *⁴For God said, 'Honor your father and mother'. . . ⁵But you say that if a man says to his father or mother, 'Whatever help you might otherwise have received from me is a gift devoted to God,' ⁶he is not to honor his father with it (Matthew 15:4-6).*

The tradition of the Pharisees, as good as it sounded, went directly against the Word of God. Jesus rebuked them for it.

A Jewish rabbi in Denver, Colorado, once told me about this practice. Many young professionals of that time came from the provinces to the city of Jerusalem to study, leaving their parents in the province. They found work in the city and had good incomes. They neglected to send support to their parents, but knowing the commandment of God, felt guilty about it. So, they did what many religious people do, and went to their priest for advice. "What shall we do? Do we have to send help to our parents?" The priests told them that if they would do three things, they would not have to give support to their parents:

1. Go to the temple.
2. Pay the tithe (10% of the gross income) to the priest.
3. Ask God's blessing on the 90% that remains.

Money that is blessed becomes *corban*, a Hebrew word meaning "devoted to God." Once the money is *corban*, the individual may use it as he wishes (Mark 7:11).

The advice of the Pharisees, as good as it sounded, went directly against the Word of God. So Jesus said,

> *Thus you nullify the word of God for the sake of your tradition (Matthew 15:4b).*

The Pharisees had come between God and the people with an interpretation, a tradition, that clearly contradicted God's Word. While they claimed to teach God's Word, they led people astray from it. Jesus continued:

> *[7]You hypocrites! Isaiah was right when he prophesied about you: [8]"These people honor me with their lips, but their hearts are far from me. [9]They worship me in vain; their teachings are but rules taught by men" (Matthew 15:7-9).*

These words were spoken to religious leaders among those who claimed to worship the true God —

God's truth is revealed in His written Word, the Bible.

the God of Abraham, Isaac, and Jacob. Jesus referred to their traditions as "rules taught by men," and to the Scriptures as "the Word of God." He strongly condemned the scribes and Pharisees for violating the Word of God in order to keep their traditions. Jesus believed the truth was in the Scriptures, not in the traditions of the church.

The Teaching of the Apostles Concerning Final Authority

Jesus' apostles after Him also taught that the Scriptures are God's very Word, and, therefore, they are true.

The Bible has God for its author and nobody can contradict it.
The Bible must be the FINAL AUTHORITY in matters of faith and practice.

Peter said:

Prophecy never had its origin in the will of man, but men spoke from God as they were carried along by the Holy Spirit (2 Peter 1:21).

Paul said:

All Scripture is God-breathed and is useful for teaching, rebuking, correcting, and training in righteousness (2 Timothy 3:16).

Rules Taught by Men or Commands of God?

The Catholic Church teaches that it is a sin to eat meat on Fridays of Lent. Those who do lose sanctifying grace. This rule is binding in conscience. They teach, in effect, that the road to salvation and eternal life requires compliance with this human tradition.

The following Scripture passages speak to this kind of regulation:

[8]See to it that no one takes you captive through hollow and deceptive philosophy, which depends on human tradition and the basic principles of this world rather than on Christ . . . [9]For in Christ all the fullness of Deity lives in bodily form, . . . [20]Since you died with Christ to the basic principles of this world, why, as though you still belonged to it, do you submit to its rules: "Do not handle!

Do not taste! Do not touch!"? . . . [22]These are all destined to perish with use, because they are based on human commands and teachings. [23]Such regulations indeed have an appearance of wisdom, with their self-imposed worship, their false humility and their harsh treatment of the body, but they lack any value in restraining sensual indulgence (Colossians 2:8, 9, 20, 22, 23).

[1]The Spirit clearly says that in the later times some will abandon the faith and follow deceiving spirits and things taught by demons. [2]Such teachings come through hypocritical liars, whose consciences have been seared as with a hot iron. [3]They forbid people to marry and order them to abstain from certain foods, which God created to be received with thanksgiving by those who believe and who know the truth. [4]For everything God created is good, and nothing is to be rejected if it is received with thanksgiving, [5]because it is consecrated by the word of God and prayer (1 Timothy 4:1-5).

The Bible clearly teaches that salvation is through Christ alone, and that those who are in Christ are no longer guided by human traditions, commands, and teachings. Every false teaching that comes from man originates with the evil one and evil spirits. Such teachings may include forbidding people to marry or to eat certain foods at certain times.

Based on the Scriptures quoted above, what do you think about a rule that says it is a sin to eat meat on Fridays of Lent? Mark those statements below which you believe to be true according to the Scriptures.

_____ The rule is clearly a command from God.

_____ The rule is being taught by men, but not by the Word of God.

_____ The rule has an appearance of wisdom because it is healthy not to eat meat all the time, but it has no eternal consequence.

____ Those who forbid people to eat certain foods are teaching a doctrine of demons.

Nullifying the Word of God for the Sake of Tradition?

Compare the biblical version of the Ten Commandments with that in the Catholic catechisms. Notice, as pointed out in the testimony at the beginning of this chapter, that the catechisms omit the second commandment.

The Ten Commandments from Catholic Catechisms	The Ten Commandments from the Jerusalem Bible (Exodus 20:3-17)
1. You shall worship the Lord your God and Him only shall you serve.	1. You shall have no gods except me.
2. You shall not take the name of the Lord your God in vain.	2. **You shall not make yourself a carved image.**
3. Remember the Sabbath day, to keep it holy.	3. You shall not utter the name of Yahweh your God to misuse it.
4. Honor your father and your mother.	4. Remember the Sabbath day and keep it holy.
5. You shall not kill.	5. Honor your father and your mother.
6. You shall not commit adultery.	6. You shall not kill.
7. You shall not steal.	7. You shall not commit adultery.
8. You shall not bear false witness.	8. You shall not steal.
9. You shall not covet your neighbor's wife.	9. You shall not bear false witness.
10. You shall not covet your neighbor's goods.	10. You shall not covet.

Consider the following statement from former Catholic priest, Robert A. Champagne:

> *Often people have asked me if I had studied and read the Bible either as a seminarian or a priest, and if so why hadn't I seen the truth? First of all, the unregenerated man cannot see the light (1 Corinthians 2:14). And secondly, in the Roman Catholic system, tradition is on an equal par with the Bible itself. This was affirmed at both the Council of Trent and the Second Vatican Council, which stated that "The Church does not draw her certainty about all revealed truth from the Holy Scriptures alone" (Vatican II, Constitution on Divine Revelation-paragraph 9).*
>
> *In spite of the fact that the Word of God clearly contradicts such practices and institutions as the Mass, the papacy, the priesthood, prayer to the saints, confession to a man, prayers for the dead, crucifixes and images, etc., Roman Catholic tradition upholds them even at the expense of twisting the Scriptures, changing them, or omitting a part of them. Consider the Roman Catholic Institution's omission of the Second Commandment in order to freely promote idolatry . . . .*

Conclusion

♦ Which of the following statements do you believe accurately represents the convictions and teaching of Jesus concerning Scripture and tradition?

    ____ Traditions are rules taught by men, but the Scriptures are the Word of God.

    ____ Traditions have equal authority with the Word of God.

♦   If a tradition of your church contradicts the clear teaching of Scripture, which would you choose to obey?

_____ I would choose to obey the Scriptures.

_____ I would choose to obey the traditions of my church.

♦   Why would you make that choice?

♦   What do you think Jesus would say to those who have thus tampered with the Ten Commandments?

_____ "You nullify the Word of God for the sake of your tradition!"

_____ "It is O.K. The second commandment is not needed anyway."

_____ "Thanks. Your modifications are an improvement on the old law."

_____ "You honor me with your lips, but your hearts are far from me."

_____ "Your teachings are but rules taught by men."

♦   Write a brief prayer to God in the space provided below, asking Him to give you proper respect and reverence for His Holy Word.

_____

_____

_____

_____

_____.

Chapter 2

The Truth About Salvation Part I

While studying theology in England I began to have serious doubts concerning certain doctrines of my church which I found difficult to reconcile with Scripture. These doubts continued to trouble me even after my ordination, but I endeavored to smother them by plunging into my studies and teaching assignments. My schedule was so heavy that there was little time for research or prayer.

After ten years of hard work I returned to my home in Italy for a year of rest and recuperation. My doubts revived and increased in number, as did my determination to find satisfactory solutions to the doctrines troubling my spirit. I read incessantly and pondered deeply the works of our great theologians, but all my doubts persisted, some stronger than ever before.

Upon returning to the Philippines, I remember laying aside all my books of theology. I was determined to focus full attention on a single Book, the Word of God, particularly the

New Testament. The Bible became my only source of wisdom for preaching, teaching, meditation and reading. In a relatively short time, my doubts began to disappear as one after another was solved by my study of the Scriptures.

At the end of January 1974, I was in Santa Cruz, Laguna, south of Manila, where an attractive Baptist church had just been built. I had never been in a Protestant church, so I walked quietly into the sanctuary to look around. Almost immediately I was greeted by a friendly Christian believer who insisted upon introducing me to the pastor, Rev. Ernesto Montealegre, a most wonderful man of God.

We talked together for a couple of hours, I doing all I could to make him a good Catholic, and he quietly answering all my questions. Of course, I did not succeed in converting him to Catholicism; but neither did he convert me to Protestantism. Nevertheless, many of his answers struck me with great force, so that at the end of two hours, I left with multiplied doubts in my heart. From that day on, a period of Calvary started for me: sleepless nights, agonizing indecision and a frightening lack of courage to profess the truth of Scripture. Gradually I began to see what the Truth was, but I did not know what I was to do—until the night of February 20, 1974.

That night I was alone in my room, and for the first time in my life, I truly prayed. I asked Christ to take over because I didn't know what to do. For the first time I felt I was the chief of sinners. But what kind of sinner, you might ask? Well, to be perfectly honest, I never smoked, got drunk or broke my vows of celibacy throughout all the years I was active in the priesthood. I left no bad record behind me, but was rather proud of my achievements as a religious priest. In fact, my sin was my pride. It was a pride which would not let Christ come into my life because of what my bishop and superior might think or say. I kept asking myself, "If you accept Christ alone as your Savior and Lord, what will your superiors say? What will your colleagues think, or your students? They esteem you; how can you betray them?" I lacked the courage to be honest with these people; the esteem of men meant more to me than love for the Truth. But then, as I was praying, my eyes fell upon the text in John's Gospel which reads:

> ⁴²*Even then, many Jewish authorities believed in Jesus; but because of the Pharisees they did not talk about it openly, so as not to be expelled from the synagogue.* ⁴³*They loved the approval of men rather than the approval of God (John 12:42, 43, Good News Bible).*

Those last words penetrated my heart like a sharp, two-edged sword, but they also filled me with strength and courage. I was set free! That night I slept without the pain and agonizing indecision of those terrible weeks.

The following morning as I awoke, the picture of that kindly Baptist pastor came to mind. I dressed hastily and drove to his church where we talked together for some time. He gave me some tracts and pamphlets which I gladly accepted. Then turning rather quickly as we were parting I asked: *"In case I leave my church, may I come to stay with you? Will you accept me?"* He smiled saying, *"We have a room here and the believers will take care of you."*

It took me six days of prayer and more reading before making my decision. On February 26th I accepted Christ as my personal Savior and Lord. I invited Him to take over the direction of my life as I was leaving everything behind me: my car, my library, all my possessions. I wrote my letter of resignation to the superior and went to live with my new-found spiritual friends in Santa Cruz.

On March 3rd at 11:00 a.m. I publicly confessed my evangelical faith and was baptized in the Santa Cruz River which flows behind the church. From the day I accepted Christ to this very moment, I haven't had one single second of remorse, nostalgia or homesickness for my previous life. I was literally filled with joy and knew a freedom from doubt beyond all description. I remember one priest who visited me a few days later asked: *"Tony, how did you dare in just five days to make such a decision? You have left the Catholic Church—twenty centuries of culture, popes, saints, all that you have learned and loved for so very long!"* I gave him the answer which came from my heart: *"I don't think I really left anything; rather, I found everything when I found Christ."*

Introduction

In this chapter we will consider what the Bible teaches about salvation—how a person receives forgiveness of sins, is put right with God, and is given eternal life. In the next chapter, we will compare the teachings of God's Word with the teachings of the Roman Catholic Church.

THE TEACHING OF GOD'S WORD
CONCERNING SALVATION

1. **God created us all to enjoy life with Him. Life with God was lost because of sin.**

    Sin came into the world through one man, and his sin brought death with it. As a result, death has spread to the whole human race because everyone has sinned (Romans 5:12).

    • **Sin has separated us from God.**

    But your iniquities have separated you from your God . . . (Isaiah 59:2).

    • **Sin brings God's judgment.**

    [8]He will punish those who do not know God and do not obey the Gospel of our Lord Jesus. [9]They will be punished with everlasting destruction and shut out from the presence of the Lord . . . (2 Thessalonians 1:8, 9).

2. **Good works and obedience to God's commandments cannot restore what was lost.**

- **Good works cannot take away sin.**

    [8]For it is by grace you have been saved, through faith— and this is not from yourselves, it is the gift of God— [9]not by works, so that no one can boast (Ephesians 2:8, 9).

- **Obeying the Ten Commandments cannot make a person right with God.**

    A person is put right with God only through faith in Jesus Christ, never by doing what the Law requires . . . no one is put right with God by doing what the Law requires (Galatians 2:16).

3. **Only Jesus can take away our sin and make us right with God.**

    Jesus answered, "I am the way and the truth and the life. No one comes to the Father except through me" (John 14:6).

    The next day John saw Jesus . . . and said, "Look, the Lamb of God, who takes away the sin of the world!" (John 1:29).

In order to take away our sins, Jesus suffered as the Lamb of God. This idea needs some explanation.

Sin is viewed by God as a debt. The payment due for sin is death. Because God is just, the sinner cannot be released from punishment until the debt to sin is paid. Jesus came to give His life a "ransom" for many (Matthew 20:28). He paid the price of our freedom by paying our debt to sin.

In the Old Testament God established a system of sacrifices to reinforce this idea in the minds of His people. He required that animals be sacrificed as payment for sins. These animals were viewed as substitutes who died in the place of the sinner.

Before the animal was slain, the sinner symbolically transferred his sin to the animal by laying his hands on its head. The animal, then, bearing the sin of another in his body, suffered the penalty due for that sin. Every sacrifice was a reminder that the penalty for sin is death, and that the only remedy for sin is the death of a substitute.

These sacrifices could not take away sin, but they portrayed perfectly what Jesus would do as the Lamb of God (Hebrews 10:11). He died as our substitute, bearing our sin in His body, and paying the debt we owed for sin.

- **Jesus paid the penalty for sin by His death on the cross.**

    ⁵But he was pierced for our transgressions, he was crushed for our iniquities; the punishment that brought us peace was upon him . . . ⁶The Lᴏʀᴅ has laid on him the iniquity of us all (Isaiah 53:5,6).

- **Jesus rose again and gives life to those who believe in Him.**

    ²⁵Jesus said to her, "I am the resurrection and the life. He who believes in me will live, even though he dies; ²⁶and whoever lives and believes in me will never die" (John 11:25, 26).

- **Jesus will come again to take His own to their eternal home.**

    Christ was sacrificed once to take away the sins of many people; and he will appear a second time, not to bear sin, but to bring salvation to those who are waiting for him (Hebrews 9:28).

4. We can be saved only by faith in the Lord Jesus.

True faith involves trusting Christ alone for salvation. Many who say they believe in Jesus are not trusting Him completely to save them. They do not believe that Jesus alone makes them worthy of heaven, but rather that observing the sacraments and obeying the commandments of God are also necessary. They trust Christ also, but they do not trust Christ alone.

- **We must trust Christ alone, not Christ also.** To people who said they believed in Christ but trusted also in the Law for salvation, Paul writes:

  2. . . Christ is of no use to you at all . . . 4Those of you who try to be put right with God by obeying the Law have cut yourselves off from Christ (Galatians 5:2, 4 TEV).

- **We must turn from sin.**

  Repent, then, and turn to God so that your sins may be wiped out (Acts 3:19).

- **We must believe that Jesus died for our sins and rose again.**

  Believe in the Lord Jesus and you will be saved . . . (Acts 16:31).

- **We must call upon the name of the Lord Jesus, trusting Him to save us.**

  Everyone who calls on the name of the Lord will be saved (Romans 10:13).

True faith is more than knowing the facts about Jesus. It is trusting Him completely and receiving Him personally as Lord and Savior:

  To all who received Him, to those who believed in his name, he gave the right to become children of God (John 1:12).

- If you have not already done so, **you may receive Christ today** by putting your trust in Him, and calling upon Him to save you. You may want to pray something like this:

> *Father, I am a sinner. I am separated from you because of my sin. I know that you sent Jesus to save me. Right now I trust Him alone to save me, and receive Him by faith as my Savior and Lord. Please take away my sin, make me your child, and help me to live in a way that pleases you. In Jesus' name, Amen.*

Conclusion: Review what you have learned in this chapter by answering the following questions.

◆ According to Isaiah 59:2, how has sin affected our relationship to God (see p. 24)?

◆ How have you experienced alienation from God personally? Check the answers below that have been true of you.

_____ I have felt guilty because of sin.

_____ I have feared death and judgment.

_____ I have felt a need to appease God because of wrong things I have done.

_____ I do not feel acceptable to God, even though I am very religious.

_____ I have been ashamed before God because of my sinfulness.

_____ I have been angry with God.

_____ I have been disobedient to God's Law.

_____ I have experienced pain, sorrow, or sickness that is the consequence of sin.

◆ Imagine that you are a convicted criminal in God's court of justice. What could you say to persuade God that he **must** pardon you? Choose the statement below that you think is a proper ground of appeal.

_____ You have to pardon me, Lord, because I am a religious person.

_____ You have to pardon me, Lord. Sure I broke this one law of yours, **but** I have kept the others.

____ You have to pardon me, Lord. I did break this law, but I have also done many good things for people.

____ Lord, I deserve to be punished. I have done wrong. I can only appeal to your mercy and ask you for forgiveness.

Only the fourth statement above provides a legitimate ground of appeal. We cannot demand God's' forgiveness because we have been religious, tried to keep the law, or done many good deeds. The only hope for a convicted criminal in God's courtroom is an appeal to God's mercy. Good works and obedience to God's law cannot absolve our guilt or balance the scales of justice.

♦ Imagine again that you are a convicted criminal in God's court of justice. God tells you that Jesus has paid the penalty for your sin, and that if you will repent and believe, He will pardon you. How would you answer Him?

____ Lord, I know that Jesus paid for my sin. But I don't think that what He paid is enough. I will pay myself by doing penance.

____ God, I know that Jesus died for my sin. But I don't think that is enough. I want to pay for my sin with good deeds.

____ I'm sorry for my sin. Thank you for sending your Son to die in my place. Thank you for your great mercy. I believe you, and I trust you to do what you have promised.

By rejecting God's offer in Christ, we reject God's mercy. If we insist on paying for sins ourselves, then the sacrifice of Christ will be of no value to us. We must realize that we cannot pay for sins ourselves, and accept God's gift of forgiveness in Christ.

♦ **True** or **False:** Place a "T" in front of statements you know are true. Place a "F" in front of statements that are not true. Review this lesson to check your answers.

_____ Good works and obedience to God's law cannot take away sin or put a person right with God.

_____ In order to pay for our sins completely, we must believe in Jesus, keep the commandments of God, and do penance.

_____ A person is put right with God only through faith in Jesus Christ, never by doing what the Law requires.

_____ Jesus died on the cross to pay the penalty for our sins and rose again on the third day.

_____ Jesus is the resurrection and the life. All who believe in Him will never die.

♦ According to Galatians 5:2-4, what happens when a person trusts both in Christ and in the Law for salvation (see p. 27)?

♦ What does it mean to believe in Jesus (see pp. 26-27)?

Chapter 3

The Truth About Salvation Part II

O ne day, while sharing with a good Roman Catholic
priest, I asked him: *"Since you say that you have faith
in Christ, what does Jesus do for you when you believe?"*

Immediately he replied, *"He opens the gates of heaven,
which had been shut because of sin."*

"How will you enter?" I insisted.

*"By obeying the commandments of God and the precepts
of the Church after being baptized,"* he replied.

*"So Jesus opened the door, but now you must enter by
avoiding sin and doing good deeds?"* I asked.

"Exactly," was his response.

"If this is the case," I continued, *"can you really call Jesus
your Savior?"*

"What do you mean?" he questioned.

"Let me give you an illustration," I said. *"Suppose you are
in prison because of a crime, your feet are chained to the floor,*

and your hands tied. Suddenly a fire breaks out in the prison cells! Moved by compassion, one of the prison guards opens the door of your cell, and runs away. Has He saved your life? Obviously not, because you are in chains. You will still burn in the fire, because you cannot get out.

"*God's Word tells us that all men have sinned (Romans 3:23), and are in bondage, chained by sin, totally unable to make any spiritual move on their own. So Jesus, in order to save us, must do something more than open the door of heaven. He actually shatters the chains of sin, and takes us out the door, delivering us from condemnation. No one but Jesus can break the chains of sin. He does it whenever a person truly repents and accepts Him, and Him alone, as Savior.*"

Introduction

In the last chapter we considered what the Bible teaches about salvation—how a person receives forgiveness of sins, is put right with God, and is given eternal life. In this chapter, we will compare the teachings of God's Word with the teachings of the Roman Catholic Church.

OFFICIAL TEACHINGS OF CATHOLICISM THAT ARE TRUE TO THE WORD OF GOD

When we talk about Catholicism, we speak of the official Roman Catholic teaching, not about what some Roman Catholic theologians teach, or what some priests preach, or what many Catholics believe. There is only one official teaching in the Catholic Church—that which is approved by Rome, established by the Popes, and defined by the Councils, the latest being Vatican II.

Many Catholic teachings are consistent with the teaching of the Word of God. The Bible views salvation as deliverance from sin and from the consequences of it. So does the Church of Rome. This stands in opposition to "Liberation Theology" and some modern views of salvation that have entered both the Catholic and Protestant world. Rome officially teaches that Christ came to save us from sin and from eternal damnation. The salvation Catholicism teaches is not primarily liberation from poverty, from suffering, from war, from hunger, or from disease. Deliverance from these things may, at times, be a consequence of salvation. But the Popes, particularly Pope Pius XII and Pope Paul VI, on many occasions condemned Roman Catholic theologians of South America and some parts of Europe who defined salvation in terms of liberation from the hardships and injustices of life as we know it on earth. Pope Pius XII once said that if this is the kind of salvation Christ came to bring, then Jesus Himself would not have been saved because He was poor!

The Roman Catholic Church affirms the truths of Christ's death and resurrection. It also maintains that Christ came, died, and rose again, so that those who believe in Him may have everlasting life. These teachings, too, are consistent with the teachings of the Word of God.

OFFICIAL TEACHINGS OF CATHOLICISM THAT ARE CONTRARY TO THE WORD OF GOD

1. **The teaching that faith is necessary for salvation, but not sufficient**

The Bible clearly teaches that salvation is by *faith alone*. The Catholic Church teaches that salvation is by *faith*, but not by *faith alone*. Here, the Catholic Church deviates from the clear teaching of Scripture. First, let's consider what the Bible has to say:

> For we conclude that a person is put right with God only through faith, and not by doing what the Law commands (Romans 3:28, TEV).

Yet we know that a person is put right with God only through faith in Jesus Christ, never by doing what the Law requires. We, too, have believed in Christ Jesus in order to be put right with God through our faith in Christ, and not by doing what the Law requires. For no one is put right with God by doing what the Law requires (Galatians 2:16, TEV).

Contrary to what the Bible teaches, Rome asserts that while faith is absolutely necessary for salvation, it is not sufficient. Faith is necessary in that without believing in Christ, no one will be saved, though they be good and religious people. Muslims, Hindus, and Buddhists cannot be saved because they lack true faith. Up to Vatican II, even Protestants could not be saved because they, too, lacked true faith according to Rome.

Faith is not sufficient?

While faith is necessary to the Catholic, it is not sufficient; other things must be added to faith in order for a person to be saved. Christ does not actually save those who believe in Him, but only makes salvation possible. Salvation is ultimately attained through the sacraments.

• **Faith plus baptism**

One such sacrament is baptism. Baptism is absolutely necessary for salvation. There are three baptisms in the Catholic Church. A person must experience one of these three baptisms in order to be saved:

1. Baptism of water (the official sacrament)
2. Baptism of blood (martyrdom)
3. Baptism of desire (an expressed desire to be baptized prevented by untimely death)

Baptism alone *may* be sufficient to save a person from the penalty for sin, but faith alone will never be sufficient. Infants who have no faith, but have been baptized will go to heaven.

But no person who has *not* been baptized will ever go to heaven.

• **Faith plus penance**

Another sacrament, like baptism, that is necessary for salvation is the sacrament of penance, or confession to a priest. If a person commits a mortal sin and dies without confessing it to a priest, that person will go to hell, taking his faith with him.

Therefore, according to the Catholic Church, a person *cannot* be saved by faith alone. Whereas, according to the Word of God, a person can be saved *only* by faith alone.

• **Catholic Objections To the Doctrine of Salvation by Faith Alone**

There is one Bible passage usually quoted by Catholics against the biblical teaching of "salvation by faith alone." It is found in James, chapter 2, culminating with verse twenty four which says:

> *You see that a person is justified by what he does and not by faith alone.*

Both Catholics and Evangelicals believe that the Bible is the inerrant Word of God[1] and as such free from real contradictions. All who accept James 2:24 as inspired also accept the following verses of Scripture which say:

> *However, to the man who does not work but trusts God who justifies the wicked, his faith is credited as righteousness (Romans 4:5).*

---

[1]"Holy Scripture comprises the sacred books of the Old and New Testaments. These, with all their parts, are inspired by God and have Him for Author; and are, therefore, free from error, not only in moral and religious statements" (*The Teaching of the Catholic Church*), by Roos and Neuner, Jesuits; ed. Karl Rahner, Jesuit).

> *(We) know that a man is not justified by observing the law, but by faith in Jesus Christ. So we, too, have put our faith in Christ Jesus that we may be justified by faith in Christ and not by observing the law, because by observing the law no one will be justified (Galatians 2:16).*

> *You who are trying to be justified by law have been alienated from Christ (Galatians 5:4).*

> *⁸For it is by grace you have been saved through faith— and this not from yourselves, it is the gift of God—⁹not by works so that no one can boast (Ephesians 2:8, 9).*

Human reason itself teaches that if the Word of God is free from error, it contains no real contradictions. If a statement is true, a contradicting statement must be false! Since Evangelicals and Catholics accept both statements as infallibly true, they cannot be contradictory. There may be apparent contradictions, but there can be no real contradictions.

Since the Bible clearly states in many passages that salvation is by faith alone and not by works (Romans 4:1-8; Galatians 5:1-6; Romans 10:4, 11; Titus 3:5; John 3:14-17, and many more), James cannot be teaching that salvation is by works and not by faith alone. Actually, when understood in their context, James and Paul complement each other. They are answering two diffferent, yet related questions.

In Romans and Galatians Paul is answering the question, "What must I do to be saved?" He demonstrates that no one can earn merit for salvation by doing good works. Salvation is a gift of grace that God gives to those who have faith in Jesus.

James takes the next step by asking, "What does it mean to have faith?" He proves by his argument that genuine faith produces good works. Faith that does not work is not genuine. Thus, he says:

> *Show me your faith without deeds, and I will show you my faith by what I do . . . faith without deeds is useless . . . (James 2:18-20).*

Good works are the fruit of faith (James), but they are not the basis for forgiveness (Paul). Faith alone saves (Paul); and a faith that saves, works (James).

The faith we profess is useless when our works prove the contrary! James rightly speaks of the necessity of good works as evidence, proof, and result of true and living faith (James 2:12-17). James does not teach that we are justified by works (in front of God), but that good works, the fruit of true faith, justify us before men.

James and Paul complement each other. Paul himself recognizes good works as the fruit of faith. While arguing that we are not saved *by works* (Ephesians 2:8, 9), he agrees that we are saved *to do good works* (Ephesians 2:10).

2. The teaching that faith is belief without trust

The biblical word "faith" has two aspects: (1) belief and (2) trust.[2] To have faith is both to trust a person and, as a consequence, to believe what that person says. We trust persons and believe principles or ideas. Trust is in persons. Belief is in statements. Biblical faith is both trust in the person of Christ and belief in what Christ teaches. Biblical faith includes trust (Romans 4:5).

Trust is in persons.
Belief is in statements.

Rome, however, eliminated the idea of trust from faith, when at the Council of Trent, it condemned Luther's doctrine of *Fides Fiducialis* or "Trusting Faith." Yet, this is the clear teaching of the apostle Paul in his epistle to the Romans:

> *However, to the man that does not work, but **trusts** God who justifies the wicked, his faith is credited as righteousness (Romans 4:5).*

---

[2]See notes on the Greek word pistis (faith, trust, conviction) from πειθω (to persuade, be persuaded, trust) at the bottom of page 1 in the introduction to this book.

Therefore, not only Luther, but Paul himself stands condemned by the Council of Trent.

There is a huge difference between faith as belief, and faith as trust. Suppose I'm out in front of my garden washing my car. A young man whom I have never met passes by and greets me.

"Good morning, Sir!", he says. *"Have you read the newspaper this morning? The President was shot!"* (I haven't read the newspaper yet, so I have no reason not to believe the man.)

"That's shocking!" I say. *"What happened?"* (He gives me all the details. I believe him.)

Then the young man asks, *"Would you allow your teenage daughter to spend a day with me?"*

I respond, *"You and I just met. I don't know you well enough to let my daughter spend the day with you. I'm sorry, but I couldn't allow her to do that."*

I believed him, but I did not trust him.

If faith is merely belief and not trust, then even the devil believes: He knows what is true, but he does not subject himself to the lordship of Christ and he doesn't trust Him. This is the clear teaching of God's Word: *"You believe that there is one God. Good! Even the demons believe that—and shudder"* (James 2:19).

♦   In your own words, write a definition of what it means to have faith: _____

_____

_____.

The Bible teaches that it is trust in Christ, not merely belief, that saves. Many people in the Bible had faith in God; all the Jews believed in God. But salvation comes only through faith in the Savior, Jesus (Acts 4:12).

An acrobat illustrated the difference between mere belief and trust at the Niagara Falls one day. First, he walked across the falls on a tightrope pushing a wheelbarrow just to prove that he could do it. Then he asked the crowd if they believed he could push a person across the rope in the wheelbarrow. The crowd screamed "Yes," affirming their confidence in his ability. Then he asked them, "Which of you will volunteer to get into the wheelbarrow and let me push you across?" No one would. They all believed he could, but none were willing to trust him to do it.

3. The teaching that a person is saved by his own merit

If, as in Roman Catholic theology, faith is merely belief in certain ideas or statements, it is logical to conclude that faith is not enough. Thus, the Catholic Church teaches that in addition to faith, two things are needed: (1) baptism and (2) personal merit. We have already discussed baptism. Let's move on now to personal merit.

How does a person merit salvation? By keeping the Ten Commandments. If he fails to keep a commandment and falls into sin, he must immediately go to confession and do penance or else he is doomed to hell. He *must* do penance, either in this life or in the next, if he will be saved. If a person does not pay through penance, he *will* pay in purgatory. He will pay until he becomes worthy. He must merit salvation before he can receive it.

The Catholic dogmatic teaching on Purgatory is no secondary or minor doctrine, because it directly denies the sufficiency of Christ's merit for our salvation. Purgatory is supposed to be a place or state where souls are "purified" from sin and so become **Purgatory denies the sufficiency of Christ's merit.** "worthy" of heaven. Those who die without unconfessed mortal sins, but with venial sins or without doing full penance of their mortal sins, must suffer for an indefinite period of time until their sins are purged. According to this doctrine, the basis of our claim to heaven is not Christ's righteousness, but our own merit; not only the sufferings and death of Christ, but also our own.

The All-Sufficiency of Christ

While sharing with a group of Charismatic Catholics in a Bible study, I discussed with them the all-sufficiency of Christ's sacrifice as payment for our sins. Little did I know that their priest was present. He interrupted me, saying that the Bible teaches that the sufferings of Christ were not complete and sufficient, and that we must make up what is lacking by our own sufferings. Then he opened the Bible and read Colossians 1:24 where Paul writes:

> Now I rejoice in what was suffered for you, and I fill up in my flesh what is still lacking in regard to Christ's afflictions, for the sake of his body, which is the church.

I thank the Lord that the group was open to understand my answer. The phrase "what was suffered for you" is a reference to Paul's sufferings as a messenger of Christ, not Christ's sufferings as the lamb of God who takes away the sin of the world. Paul suffered, not to pay for sins, but to deliver the message of salvation through faith in Christ to those who had not heard.

In the preceding verses, just before Paul speaks of "what is still lacking in regard to Christ's afflictions," he affirms the sufficiency of Christ's death by saying:

> [21]Once you were alienated from God and were enemies in your minds because of your evil behavior. [22]But now he has reconciled you by Christ's physical body through death to present you holy in his sight, without blemish and free from accusation . . . (Colossians 1:21, 22).

While Christ's death is sufficient to reconcile us to God and to present us holy in His sight, this message must be proclaimed so that people can hear it and believe (Romans 10:13-15). Paul suffered as a servant commissioned by God to preach the Gospel to the Gentiles (Colossians 1:23). Jesus suffered to purchase our redemption; Paul suffered to proclaim it. Jesus suffered as the lamb of God; Paul suffered as a messenger of God. Jesus suffered as a sacrifice; Paul suffered as a spokesman.

The sacrifice for sin has been paid in full. Jesus completed those sufferings. The sufferings that remain are to be endured by those who preach the Gospel to all nations. Christ did not complete these kinds of sufferings, because that responsibility has been entrusted to the Church. Such a task may at times involve great suffering, as it did in the case of the apostle Paul. To suffer in this way is to fill what is still lacking in regard to Christ's afflictions (Colossians 1:25).

In many Catholic churches in Europe, there is a picture of a balance or scale on the pulpit. On the one side of the balance are sins; on the other good works or merits. This visual was used in the Middle Ages to fix this idea in the minds of people: "In the end, unless your merits outweigh your sins, you have no hope."

Contrary to the teaching of the Catholic Church, the Bible teaches that salvation is a gift of God, not merited or earned, but granted <u>by grace</u> to all who trust Christ and believe.

> *8-9For it is by God's grace that you have been saved through faith. It is not the result of your own efforts [works], but God's gift, so that no one can boast about it. 10God has made us what we are, and in our union with Christ Jesus he has created us for a life of good deeds, which he has already prepared for us to do (Ephesians 2:8-10, TEV).*

> *4But when the kindness and love of God our Savior was revealed, he saved us. 5It was not because of any good deeds that we ourselves had done, but because of his own mercy that he saved us . . . (Titus 3:4, 5).*

Conclusion

Roman Catholicism teaches that *baptism, belief, and personal merit* are all necessary for salvation. The Word of God teaches that *faith* (belief-trust) is all that is necessary.

Believe in the Lord Jesus and you will be saved (Acts 16:31).

The Bible is clear in its teaching. Baptism does not confer grace, it is an act of obedience, a testimony to faith (Acts 2:41). Good works do not bring merit; they are expressions of obedience, the fruit of faith (James 2:17, 18).

♦ Which of the following statements is true according to Galatians 2:16, TEV (see p. 35)?

___ People are put right with God because they believe and keep the Ten Commandments.

___ People are put right with God because they obey the Ten Commandments.

___ People are put right with God only because they believe in Christ.

♦ According to Ephesians 2:8-10, which of the following statements is true (see p. 41)?

___ People are saved by good works.

___ People are saved by faith and good works.

___ People are saved by faith alone, not by works.

___ People are saved to do good works.

♦ According to Titus 3:4, 5, which of the following statements are true (see p. 41)?

___ God saves those who merit salvation because of their many good deeds.

___ God saves us, not because we deserve it, but because He is kind, loving, and merciful.

___ Faith in Christ only makes it possible for us to merit salvation.

___ Jesus opened the gates of heaven to us, but we must work to enter them.

___ Jesus opened the gates of heaven, and carried us through them.

♦ How would you characterize your faith in Jesus?

___ I have believed the teachings about Jesus, but I have not trusted Him to save me.

___ I have believed the teachings about Jesus, and I have trusted Him to save me.

___ I have not believed the teachings about Jesus.

Chapter 4

The Truth About Salvation Part III

> *In reply Jesus declared,*
> *"I tell you the truth,*
> *no one can see the kingdom of God*
> *unless he is born again."*
> *(John 3:3)*

*I*n the Philippines in the 1980's and early 1990's, many Roman Catholic priests taught that Jesus did not teach the necessity of being born *again*, but of being born *from above*. They insisted on this distinction in an attempt to warn Catholics against certain Charismatic groups, popularly called "the born-agains." They argued that the primary meaning of the Greek word that Jesus used is not *"again,"* but *"from above."* Thus, The Jerusalem Bible translates the phrase *"born again"* as *"born* *from above":*

> *Jesus answered, "I tell you most solemnly, unless a man is born from above, he cannot see the kingdom of God" (John 3:3).*

Actually, the Greek word used by Jesus in His conversation with Nicodemus can be translated either *"again"* or *"from above,"* depending on the context.[1] Nicodemus' response to Jesus would indicate that he understood Jesus to mean *"again"* or *"a second time":*

> *"How can a man be born when he is old?" Nicodemus asked. "Surely he cannot enter* **a second time** *in his mother's womb to be born!" (John 3:4).*

What he did not understand was the nature of this second birth—that it would be a spiritual birth, a birth that is "of the spirit." It doesn't matter which translation is used because both statements are true: A person must be born again *and* from above if he is to enter the kingdom of heaven. Either translation communicates the necessity of a *second birth.*

No one can doubt the necessity of being born again in order to enter the kingdom of God. Jesus Himself stated it three times in the third chapter of the Gospel of John. John repeats the statement in the first chapter of his Gospel and in his first epistle. Peter expresses the same truth in his first letter. The expressions *"born again," "born from above," "born of God,"* and *"born of the Spirit"* are perfect synonyms. Jesus made it very clear in His conversation with Nicodemus that to be born again one must trust or believe in Jesus for forgiveness of sins and for eternal life (John 3:3, 5, 7, 15-17).

---

[1]ανωθεν: 1. Locally from above. 2. Temporally—a. from the beginning. b. for a long time. 3. Again, anew. Walter Bauer, *(A Greek-English Lexicon of the New Testament and Other Early Christian Literature)*, Revised and augmented by FW Gingrich and Frederick Danker, (Chicago: University of Chicago Press, 1979).

Comparing the Teaching of the Catholic Church with the teaching of the Word of God

A simple comparison will show the contrast between the clear teaching of God's Word and the teaching of the Catholic Church concerning how a person is born again.

The Word of God	The Teaching of the Catholic Church
Yet to all who received Him, to those who *believed* in his name, he gave the right to become children of God—children born not of natural descent . . . but born of God. (John 1:12, 13, NIV).	*Baptism*, the gate to the sacraments, necessary for salvation, by which men and women are freed from their sins, are reborn [born again] as children of God and, configured to Christ by an indelible character, are incorporated in the Church, is validly conferred only by washing with true water together with the required form of words. (New Code of the Roman Catholic Canon Law, 1983).

Both God's Word and the Catholic Church speak of the necessity of receiving forgiveness of sins and being born again as children of God. However, they teach two different ways for accomplishing this. God's Word teaches that a person is born again through *faith* in Christ. The Catholic Church teaches that a person is born again by *baptism*.

Born of Water

One reason Catholics believe that a person is born again by baptism is the Roman Catholic interpretation of the phrase "born of water," which Jesus used in talking with Nicodemus about the new birth:

> *I tell you the truth, unless a man is **born of water** and the Spirit, he cannot enter the Kingdom of God (John 3:5).*

Roman Catholics are taught that the expression "born of water" refers to baptism. They often appeal to this verse in defense of their conviction that baptism is the sacrament by which men are "reborn as children of God." If the phrase "born of water" does refer to baptism, then their convictions are justified. What did Jesus mean by this expression? There are several different interpretations:

1.   Born of water is a reference to spiritual cleansing from sin. One possible interpretation is that to be born of water is to be cleansed from sin by the Holy Spirit. The Old Testament frequently uses water as a symbol of cleansing (Numbers 19:20, 21; Psalm 51:2; Isaiah 4:4; Zechariah 13:1). There is one messianic passage in Ezekiel 36 that may well have been in the mind of Jesus as he talked with Nicodemus late into the night. Since Nicodemus was a Pharisee and familiar with the Old Testament Scriptures, he also would have been familiar with this passage:

> *[25]I will sprinkle clean water on you, and you will be clean; I will cleanse you from all your impurities and from all your idols. [26]I will give you a new heart and put a new spirit in you; I will remove from you your heart of stone and give you a heart of flesh. [27]And I will put my Spirit in you and move you to follow my decrees and be careful to keep my laws (Ezekiel 36:25-27).*

The following chart identifies some obvious parallels between the prophecy of Ezekiel concerning the new covenant and the coming of the kingdom, and the words of Jesus to Nicodemus concerning how a person can enter the kingdom of God.

Ezekiel 36:25-27	John 3:5, 6	Interpretation
"I will sprinkle clean water on you . . . I will cleanse you from all your impurities."	"No one can enter the kingdom of God unless he is born of water . . ."	All who enter the kingdom of God will have been cleansed from all sin.
"I will give you a new heart, and put a new spirit within you . . ."	"No one can see the kingdom of God unless he is born again . . ."	"All who enter the kingdom of God will have been made new in their spirit . . ."
"I will put my Spirit in you, and move you to follow my decrees . . ."	"No one can see the kingdom of God unless he is born of water and the Spirit . . ."	Cleansing from sin and the new birth is the work of the Spirit of God.

Water is also a symbol of cleansing in the New Testament (Ephesians 5:26; Hebrews 10:22). One thing God does in saving a person is to wash his sins away (1 Corinthians 6:11; Titus 3:5).

By using the phrase "born of water and the Spirit"[2], Jesus taught that unless one is spiritually clean and pure, he cannot enter the kingdom of God, and this cleansing can be only the work of the Holy Spirit.

---

[2]The phrase "born of water and Spirit" in the original Greek language can possibly be translated "born of the Spirit as of water." It is a common case of comparison, expressed with two nouns. Another example of this kind of comparison is found in Matthew 3:11 where John says that he baptizes with water, but that Jesus will baptize "with the Holy Spirit and with fire" or "with the Holy Spirit as with fire." The meaning of the phrase "born of water and the Spirit" is that the Spirit cleanses spiritually in the same way that water does physically.

2. "Born of water" is an idiomatic expression referring to physical birth. A second possible interpretation is that John 3:6, *"Flesh gives birth to flesh, but the Spirit gives birth to spirit,"* is an explanation of the phrase "born of water and the spirit" in John 3:5. Thus, "born of water" is a reference to physical birth, and "born of spirit" to spiritual birth. In order to enter the kingdom of heaven, a person must be born twice. He must be born physically (of the flesh) and then spiritually (of the spirit).

The unborn child in the mother's womb literally lives in water. The rupture of the water sac is a sign of physical birth. In parts of Greece and southern Italy today, people will idiomatically refer to a woman about to give birth as one who is "losing water."

Some minor manuscripts have the word "For" at the beginning of verse six: *"For that which is born of flesh is flesh and that which is born of Spirit is spirit."* If verse 6 began in this way, this would be the most probable interpretation. Unfortunately, none of the most reliable manuscripts have the word "for," so that such an interpretation remains possible, but not sure.

3. Water refers to a cleansing by the Word of God. Some believe that water refers to the Word of God which brings conviction and leads to repentance and faith. They quote the apostle Peter who said:

> For you have been born again, not of perishable seed, but of imperishable, through the living and enduring word of God (1 Peter 1:23).

Paul says that faith comes by hearing the Word of Christ (Romans 10:17). Jesus Himself said:

> You are already clean because of the word I have spoken to you (John 15:3).

Some see this cleansing to be a true repentance in response to the Word of God that accompanies faith and brings about spiritual rebirth.

4.   Water is a reference to baptism. As we have already mentioned, Roman Catholics (along with Greek Orthodox and others) understand water to refer to the sacrament of baptism. The only baptism known at that time was the baptism of John. Jesus makes no reference to John's baptism in this passage. Probably Nicodemus knew about such baptism, but he would have been more familiar with the Old Testament references to water as a symbol of spiritual cleansing. If by "born of water," Jesus meant that baptism was necessary for salvation, we would expect Jesus to explain further. *This fourth interpretation is not only improbable, but it contradicts the clear teaching of the Word of God that salvation is by faith in Christ alone.*

The Teaching of Jesus about the New Birth

Jesus taught consistently that eternal life is granted to those who believe in Jesus, not to those who are baptized.

> ¹⁶*For God so loved the world that he gave his one and only Son, that whoever believes in him shall not perish but have eternal life.* ¹⁷*For God did not send his Son into the world to condemn the world, but to save the world through him.* ¹⁸*Whoever believes in him is not condemned, but whoever does not believe stands condemned already because he has not believed in the name of God's one and only Son . . . .* ³⁶*Whoever believes in the Son has eternal life, but whoever rejects the Son will not see life, for God's wrath remains on him (John 3:16-18, 36).*

> *I tell you the truth, whoever hears my word and believes him who sent me has eternal life and will not be condemned; he has crossed over from death to life (John 5:24, TEV).*

For my Father's will is that everyone who looks to the Son and believes in him shall have eternal life, and I will raise him up at the last day (John 6:40).

God gives eternal life to those who believe in Jesus (John 3:15, 16, 18, 36). Jesus taught what it means to believe with an illustration from the Old Testament:

14Just as Moses lifted up the snake in the desert, so the Son of Man must be lifted up, 15that everyone who believes in him may have eternal life (John 3:14, 15).

The illustration comes from the Israelites' wanderings in the wilderness after they had been delivered out of Egypt through the Red Sea. The Israelites were complaining about the limited supply of food and water in the desert. They doubted God's love and His ability to provide for their needs. They grumbled at God for bringing them into the desert "to die," and they whimpered about the taste of the manna God sent from heaven.

Because of their rebellion, God sent snakes, fangs full of poison, to execute judgment. Many Israelites died (See Numbers 21:8-9). Out of His great mercy, God provided a remedy for anyone who would believe and receive it. He commanded Moses to make a bronze snake and put it up on a pole, and promised that anyone who looked at it would live. Some may have tried desperately to get rid of the venom from their systems. But only those who believed God's Word through Moses, and looked at the bronze snake lifted up by Moses, were actually healed and saved.

The parallel Jesus intended to draw is clear:

The Old Testament Illustration	The New Testament Equivalent
Rebellious Israelites	All human beings
Bitten by venomous snakes causing physical death	Affected by sin causing spiritual death
Were saved, not by trying one's best, but by believing God's Word, looking with faith at the serpent	Are saved, not by trying one's best, but by believing God's Word and looking with faith to Jesus

What is the relationship in John chapter three between being born again (verse 3) and receiving eternal life (verses 16-18, 36)?

In John chapter three, Jesus drew a parallel between the way physical life begins and the way spiritual life begins. We are born physically into this world, and in the same way, we are born spiritually into the kingdom of God (John 3:3, 5). Those who are born again receive **eternal** life just as those who are born naturally receive **physical** life. A person is born again and receives eternal life when he believes in Jesus (John 3:15, 16).

There is absolutely nothing one can or must do in order to deserve physical life. It is completely a *gift* of God through one's parents. Likewise salvation or eternal life is completely a *gift* of God through Jesus Christ. It is not merited nor earned:

> *He saved us, not because of the righteous things we had done, but because of his mercy. He saved us by the washing of rebirth and renewal by the Holy Spirit (Titus 3:5).*

♦ According to the verse quoted above, why does God forgive our sins and give us new birth? Choose the best answer from the statements below.

_____ He forgives our sin and gives us new life because we have done many righteous things.

_____ He forgives our sin and gives us new life because of His great mercy.

_____ He forgives our sin and gives us new life because we are worthy and deserve it.

Conclusion

Apart from Christ, though we are alive physically, we are dead spiritually—we have physical life, but we do not have spiritual nor eternal life. Through the death and resurrection of Christ, God has made eternal life available to all who are alive physically. It is offered, but it is not imposed. Therefore, it must be received:

> *Yet to all who received him, to those who believed in his name, he gave the right to become children of God (John 1:12, NIV).*

♦ What does Jesus say in John 3:3 about how a person enters the kingdom of God?

♦ What does Jesus teach about how a person receives eternal life (see p. 50)?

♦ Have you received the gift of eternal life?

_____ I have been baptized, but I do not know for sure if I have eternal life.

_____ I have received the Lord Jesus by faith, and I am sure that I have eternal life.

_____ I want to receive Jesus and His gift of eternal life right now.

If you want to receive the gift of eternal life, you may do so by simply calling upon the Lord in prayer. You may want to review pages 21 to 30 before you pray.

Father, I am a sinner. I am separated from you because of my sin. I know that you sent Jesus to save me. Right now I trust Him alone to save me, and receive Him by faith as my Savior and Lord. Please take away my sin, make me your child, and help me to live in a way that pleases you. In Jesus' name, Amen.

Chapter 5

The Truth About Indulgences

*I*n the Roman Catholic seminary, we were encouraged to gain as many indulgences as possible for forgiveness of the penalty of sin; not just our own sin, but also for those of the *poor holy souls in purgatory*. I searched through my images or *estampitas* to find prayers and practices that would obtain partial or plenary indulgence.

Every year, on the second of August, we seminarians spent practically the whole day going in and out of the chapel reciting prayers. On that day every year the pope gives a plenary indulgence for each time one enters a church and recites the Lord's prayer, the "Hail Mary" and the "Glory Be" six times each. We believed that every time we entered and prayed, one soul went from purgatory to heaven!

Indulgences are not a practice nor doctrine of the Middle Ages only. Although some exaggerations about outright buying heaven are now avoided by the Church of Rome, the substance of their teaching about indulgences remains the same.

Statements From Vatican Council II
About Indulgences:

The doctrine of indulgences and their practice have been in force for many centuries in the Catholic Church. They would appear to be solidly founded on divine revelation (Matthew 28:18), handed down from the apostles.

These truths have been taught by the bishops, who are the successors of the apostles, and by the Roman Pontiffs, who, as successors of St. Peter, are first and foremost among the bishops.

The truth has been divinely revealed that sins are followed by punishment. God's holiness and justice inflict them. Sins must be expiated (paid for through suffering). This may be done on this earth through the sorrows, miseries and trials of this life and above all through death. Otherwise, the expiation must be made in the next life through the fire and torments of purifying punishments.

The doctrine of purgatory clearly demonstrates that even when the guilt of sin has been taken away, punishment for it or the consequences of it remain to be expiated or cleansed. In fact, in purgatory the souls of those who died in the charity (love) of God and truly repentant, but who had not made satisfaction with adequate penance for their sins and omissions, are cleansed after death with punishments designed to purge away their debt.

The Treasury of the Church is the infinite value, which can never be exhausted, which Christ's merits have before God . . . . This treasury includes, as well, the prayers and good works of the Blessed Virgin Mary. These are truly immense . . . . In the treasury, too, are the prayers and good works of all the saints . . . .

For these reasons a perennial link of charity exists between the faithful who have already reached their heavenly home, those who are expiating their sins in purgatory and those who are still pilgrims on earth. Between them there is, too, an abundant exchange of all the goods by which Divine Justice is placated so expiation is made for all the sins of the whole Mystical Body.[1]

The Basis of the Church's Teaching on Indulgences

There are three foundations upon which the doctrine of indulgences rest:
  (1) Tradition
  (2) The authority of the Church
  (3) The doctrine of purgatory

The doctrine of indulgences has no biblical basis whatsoever. The only verse of Scripture cited in the notes of the Vatican document is Matthew 28:18:

Then Jesus came to them [11 disciples] and said: "All authority in heaven and on earth has been given to me."

They appeal to this verse, not to prove the doctrine itself, but to prove their right or authority to teach it. Jesus gave the eleven authority to make disciples, baptize, and teach obedience to all that He had commanded (Matthew 28:19, 20). He did not, nor will He ever, give anyone the authority to teach doctrines that are contrary to the Word of God!

The doctrines of purgatory and indulgences are interconnected. Indulgences are one way of paying the penalty for sin; suffering in purgatory is another. The Catholic Church appeals to the doctrine of purgatory to validate the practice

---

[1]*(Vatican Council II,* 1981 edition, by Austin Flannery, O.P., pp. 62-69: selections).

of indulgences. However, the doctrine of purgatory itself is diametrically opposed to the teaching of God's Word. Purgatory is said to be a place where people pay for sins through suffering until they are clean and worthy of heaven. But the Word of God says that Jesus paid in full for both the guilt and the penalty of our sins, that His sacrifice is sufficient to make us clean and worthy of heaven, and that no other sacrifice is acceptable.

> [12]*But when this priest [Jesus] had offered for all time one sacrifice for sins, he sat down at the right hand of God ... because by one sacrifice he has made perfect forever those who are being made holy ...* [17]*"Their sins and lawless acts I will remember no more."* [18]*And where these have been forgiven, there is no longer any sacrifice for sin (Hebrews 10:12-18).*

Any payment offered for sin other than the sacrifice of Jesus (whether indulgences or suffering in purgatory) is not only unnecessary, but it is unacceptable to God and a sign of a lack of trust in Christ. Jesus Christ is the only atoning sacrifice for sins (1 John 2:1, 2).

What Are Indulgences?

In the chapters on salvation we have seen how Catholicism teaches that acceptability to God depends on our own merit, rather than on the person and finished work of Christ. Because of our sinfulness, it is admittedly very difficult for a person to become truly acceptable to God. Indulgences are Rome's way of helping out.

The Catholic Church teaches that when a person confesses his sin to a priest, the priest forgives his sin in the name of God. Upon absolution by the priest, the guilt of mortal sins is forgiven and the penitent is saved from hell. However, also upon absolution, the eternal penalty for sin is changed into temporal punishment. This temporal punishment cannot be remitted by the priest, but must be suffered by the penitent either in this world or in purgatory. In other words, a satisfactory confession and absolution by the priest saves the penitent from hell, but does not release him from temporal punishment.

Temporal punishment for sin is remitted either through suffering in purgatory, or through what the Catholic Church calls *indulgences.* The Baltimore Catechism defines an indulgence as follows:

> *An indulgence is the remission in whole or in part of the temporal punishment due to sin . . . There are two kinds of indulgences—plenary and partial . . . . A plenary indulgence is the full remission of the temporal punishment due to sin . . . . A partial indulgence is the remission of a part of the temporal punishment due to sin . . . . To gain an indulgence we must be in the state of grace (the result of a satisfactory confession to a priest) and perform the works enjoined.*

The Church teaches that the Pope is the dispenser of a vast treasury of unused merits which have been accumulated through the sufferings of Christ, the works of Mary, and the works of all saints who have done more good deeds than were required for their own personal salvation. The Church claims to be able to withdraw merits from that treasury and to apply them to any member of the church who needs it. The Pope distributes these merits through indulgences. Indulgences are usually obtained through prayers, gifts or services rendered to the Church, or as a reward for other good deeds.

The underlying assumption of the Catholic Church with regard to indulgences is that Christ's death is not sufficient for the forgiveness of sins. In addition to the sufferings of Christ, the penitent or some other sinner must also suffer punishment (expiation) if the penitent will be saved.

The Scriptures, however, clearly teach that Christ's death is sufficient payment for sin:

> *22This righteousness from God [that is needed for heaven] comes through faith in Jesus Christ to all who believe. There is no difference, 23for all have sinned and fall short of the glory of God, 24and are justified freely by His grace through the redemption that came by Christ Jesus. 25God presented him as a sacrifice of atonement, through faith in his blood (Romans 3:22-25). [Emphasis mine.]*

Two Kinds of Indulgences: Partial and Plenary

Partial indulgences, as the word suggests, remit only part of the temporal punishment due to sin. Most indulgences specify 300 days or seven years. Partial indulgences can be granted by the Pope or by bishops. Three hundred days or seven years is not the length of time by which a person's stay in purgatory is shortened. Nobody knows for sure how many hours, days, or years of suffering are averted by such an indulgence. A 300 day indulgence only means that the amount of temporal punishment remitted (or the amount of time in purgatory averted) is the same as if one had done penance and prayed for 300 days.

The Application of Indulgences

A plenary indulgence is the forgiveness of all temporal punishment. It can be granted only by the Pope. One plenary indulgence is sufficient to send one soul from purgatory to heaven, however long that soul is supposed to stay in purgatory.

Indulgences can never be applied to other living people. They can be applied only to oneself or to the dead in purgatory.

Some indulgences can *be applied ONLY to self.* If partial, these indulgences lessen one's time in purgatory after death. If plenary, they enable one to go straight to heaven—provided he does not sin again before he dies.

Other indulgences are *applicable ONLY to the dead.* Examples of such indulgences are the masses said on November 2 (All Souls' Day) and August 2 (Portiuncula). If these indulgences are partial, some time is deducted from a particular soul in purgatory. If the indulgence is plenary, a soul should immediately be delivered from purgatory and moved to heaven no matter how long that soul is supposed to spend in the place of suffering.

Finally, some indulgences are *applicable either to oneself or to the souls in purgatory.* It is left to the choice of the individual, or God decides according to the most pressing need!

Forgiveness For Sale

In 1993 I had the opportunity of visiting the Vatican with my family. A believer, a member of our Conservative Baptist Church in Rome, invited me to see something interesting in a store selling books and souvenirs beside St. Peter's Basilica. How surprised I was at seeing a priest, seated at a desk, selling pieces of paper that looked like diplomas. Each one had been signed by Pope John Paul II and declared a plenary indulgence or total forgiveness of the penalty of sins for those Catholics who bought them. They sold for $20.00 or 30,000 lires each! I was dumbfounded! I thought that the buying of indulgences had ceased with the Middle Ages!

Unlike the Middle Ages, most indulgences appropriated today are not bought and sold directly. But many do involve monetary exchanges, such as the purchase of images or prayer beads that are used for prayer and penance. The most blatant form of "selling" indulgences still being practiced today is the stipend being received by the Church to secure a mass for the living or for the dead. No priest is allowed to celebrate the sacrifice of the mass unless an intention/stipend has been given.

A mass said for the dead gains a plenary indulgence. The soul for whom the mass is offered is supposed to be released from purgatory and sent to heaven—unless, of course, the soul is already in heaven or hell. Although one mass is supposed to gain a plenary indulgence, priests often accept stipends and say masses for the same soul year after year.

When I was studying in England, I questioned my professor about this.

"If one Mass is a plenary indulgence applicable to the dead, and therefore, sufficient to send a soul from purgatory to heaven, how is it that we allow the faithful to keep offering masses for the same soul month after month, year after year?"

"There might be souls in greater need than the one we pray for," he said, *"and that would have precedence in God's eyes!"*

His answer troubled me for years. A priest is supposed to accept payment for a mass, knowing that it is not going to accomplish what the giver wishes by it, on the grounds that it will help someone else?! Is that not dishonest? Should we not be honest enough to respect the designation of a gift?! I would think that God is!

In 1975, while studying at Denver Seminary, a Filipino Catholic friend invited me to be present at his child's infant baptism at the St. Pius X parish in that city. After the short ceremony, I spoke with the Swiss parish priest. From the violet color of the vestments previously used at mass, I knew he had been celebrating a mass for the dead. I asked him if he believed in purgatory. As a liberated priest, he said he did not.

"Why then, did you say mass for the dead?" I argued. *"Those who are in heaven do not need indulgences. Those in hell cannot avail of them. So it is for the souls in purgatory you said mass!"*

"You are right," he replied, *"But it is hard to tell ordinary Catholics, who come to you with $20.00 or $50.00 and ask for*

*one more mass for their loved one, that these masses are of
no use."*

I got the message!

Peter once said to Simon the Sorcerer:

> *May your money perish with you, because you thought
> you could buy the gift of God with money (Acts 8:20)!*

♦ Do you think that the gift of God can be bought or sold?

♦ Have you or any of your Catholic friends ever paid money
for the privilege of participation in one of the sacraments
of the Church? Check which ones:

____ Mass

____ Baptism

____ Confirmation

____ Matrimony

♦ In fairness to the Catholic Church, they would deny that
they are selling forgiveness, or in the words of Martin
Luther, "trafficking in souls." However, when a priest is
given both the authority to confer grace and to collect
stipends, there is great potential for abuse. Which of the
following statements do you believe is true according to
the Scriptures? Mark each statement either *true* (T) or *false*
(F).

____ Forgiveness is free and offered by God Himself
to all who will believe.

____ Forgiveness is available in the form of indulgences
that are a part of the Church treasury and
distributed by the Pope.

____ The Church offers forgiveness to its members
through the sacraments, and has the right to
request some small contribution for its services.

♦ I have observed that the wealthy Roman Catholics in the Philippines will have many masses said for them in several different cathedrals after they die. I have also observed that the poor do not. They simply cannot afford it! Do you think that a holy God would endorse such a scheme? How does such a practice reflect on the justice of God?

♦ Which is the only condition that God requires of all that both rich and poor can equally afford?

_____ Mass
_____ Faith and repentance
_____ Indulgences
_____ Sacraments

The Truth About Forgiveness From the Word of God

The Scriptures contain a very clear and simple message about the forgiveness of sins: GOD FORGIVES ALL OUR SIN WHEN WE BELIEVE IN JESUS.

> *All the prophets testify about him that everyone who believes in him receives forgiveness of sins through his name (Acts 10:43).*

> *13. . . God made you alive with Christ. He forgave us all our sins, 14having canceled the written code, with its regulations, that was against us and that stood opposed to us; He took it away, nailing it to the cross (Colossians 2:13, 14).*

♦ What do the Scriptures teach about how a person receives forgiveness of sins (Acts 10:43)?

♦ How many of our sins are forgiven through the cross of Christ when we believe in Jesus (Colossians 2:13,14)?
_____ Only our past sins
_____ Our past and present sins
_____ All our sins, past, present, and future

Conclusion

♦ What Biblical support does the Catholic Church have for the doctrine of indulgences (see p. 56)?

♦ How are those being made holy (believers), made perfect (Hebrews 10:12-18) (see p. 57)?

♦ Once a person's sins are forgiven through the sacrifice of Jesus, what further sacrifices can be offered for sin (Hebrews 10:12-18) (see p. 57)?

♦ What can we conclude from these verses about the Catholic teaching that sins must be paid for through suffering (expiation) in purgatory (see pp. 56-59)?

♦ What does God say He will do about the sins and lawless acts of those who are made perfect forever by the sacrifice of the cross (Hebrews 10:12-18) (see p. 57)?

♦ Read Romans 3:22-25 and then mark the statement below that is ***true*** with a "**T**." Mark the statement that is ***false*** with an "**F**" (see p. 59).

_____ Christ's death is not sufficient for the forgiveness of sins. Forgiveness of sins (righteousness from God) comes only through suffering.

_____ Christ's death is sufficient for the forgiveness of sins. Forgiveness of sins comes through faith in Christ and is given *freely* to all who believe.

♦ Which of the following statements are true according to Romans 3:22-25 (see p. 59)?

_____ I must pay for my own sins through penance and suffering in order to become righteous and worthy of heaven.

_____ I do not need to pay for my sins personally, because Jesus Christ has already paid in full by His atoning sacrifice.

_____ God freely forgives and makes me righteous in Christ when I believe in him.

_____ Believing in Christ is not enough. I need indulgences in order to be completely justified and redeemed.

_____ I can be saved by the grace of God through faith in Christ alone (freely, without a single indulgence or act of penance) because of the sacrifice of Jesus.

While in Rome, our family also visited the Coliseum. There, at the entrance, I saw a cross with the words inscribed beneath it: "300 days' indulgence for anyone who kisses this cross!" Sometime during the high Middle Ages the Coliseum had been used as a Roman Catholic Church.

God does not forgive those who kiss a cross or say a rosary. The Church has no deposit of merits and no authority to dispense them—not to those who earn indulgences; not to those who pay a stipend. Offering indulgences in exchange for a stipend is trafficking in souls! God's forgiveness is not for sale.

God forgives *all* who repent and believe in Jesus. He forgives *all* of their sins. He releases them from *all* penalty, whether temporal or eternal. His forgiveness is free. The sacrifice and merit of Christ is *all*-sufficient. We need nothing more than the grace God gives when we come to Him in faith!

Chapter 6

The Truth About Holiness

One of the most positive aspects of the life I was taught to live in the Catholic seminary was the constant emphasis on the importance, beauty, and necessity of holiness. The example given us was that of the fifteen-year-old saint Dominic Savio, whose motto was "Death rather than sin." Attracted by his life of daily self-denial, penance, self-inflicted sufferings, and purity, I took him as my model. I, too, had the same motto and tried all my life to honestly keep it!

Holiness primarily meant absence of voluntary sin, much prayer, mortification, purity, kindness, love of the Eucharist, devotion to Mary and some saints, constant union with God, daily mass and communion. In order to make it to heaven, only baptism and the absence of unconfessed mortal sin at the moment of death were needed. All the rest was part of holiness or spiritual perfection, in order to avoid any time in purgatory after death, and to be as high as possible in heaven, near Jesus and Mary!

I am grateful to God for such training, which kept me from vice. It helped me stay away from many kinds of sins, especially in matters of sex where all sins were considered "mortal," or grave enough to send one to hell.

Although the "love of God" was constantly mentioned and happiness was a required characteristic to be a saint, FEAR was the foundation of my daily effort to become a saint. If I did not try my best, if I happened to fall into mortal sin and die suddenly without time to repent and confess to a priest, eternal hell awaited me. So my true motto was "Become a great saint, and that very soon!"

Holiness Needed for Heaven

God's Word teaches that holiness or perfection is required for heaven. Not even the shadow of sin can enter there!

> *Without holiness no one will see the* LORD *(Hebrews 12:14).*

God is holy. He requires holiness of His children. God's absolute holiness is the standard by which we are judged.

> *Therefore be holy, because I am holy (Leviticus 11:45).*

> *Be holy because I, the* LORD *your God, am holy (Leviticus 19:2)*

> *But just as he who called you is holy, so be holy in all you do; for it is written: "Be holy, because I am holy" (1 Peter 1:15).*

> *Be perfect as your heavenly Father is perfect (Matthew 5:48).*

Suppose you were to be graded by God's standard of holiness, would you pass or fail?

Although holiness or absolute perfection is required for heaven, the Word of God clearly states that God alone is holy!

> *For you alone are holy (Revelation 15:4).*

> *There is only one who is good (Matthew 19:17).*

None of us can come up to God's standard. We have all fallen short of His holiness.

> *For all have sinned and fall short of the glory of God (Romans 3:23).*

No one can claim to be perfect.

> *If we claim to be without sin, we deceive ourselves and the truth is not in us (1 John 1:8).*

> *If we claim we have not sinned, we make him [God] out to be a liar and his word has no place in our lives (1 John 1:10).*

Apart from God's forgiveness and grace, none of us could make it to heaven because we are not, and cannot be, as perfect and holy as God. We are all sinners.

What does the Scripture say about those who claim to be perfect (1 John 1:8, 10)?

If you cannot meet God's standard of perfection, what is your hope of eternal life?

Christ's Holiness

How does a sinner become holy? God cannot compromise His holiness and His Word. If He is to save us, He must make us holy. In His infinite wisdom and love, He found a way to do just that! He sent His one and only Son to fully pay for our sin, so that when we accept Jesus as Savior we are not only forgiven and saved, but are also sanctified and made holy.

> *. . . we have been made holy through the sacrifice of the body of Jesus Christ once for all (Hebrews 10:10).*

> *. . . so that they may receive forgiveness of sins and a place among those who are sanctified by faith in me (Acts 26:18).*

Christ's righteousness and holiness are imputed (credited) to those who truly believe in Christ. The believer is in Christ and, therefore, his claim to holiness and to eternal life, which he receives as a gift through faith, is the very righteousness and holiness of Jesus in whom there is no sin (Hebrews 4:15; John 8:46). Those who trust Christ receive forgiveness of sins and salvation because of Christ's substitutionary death and resurrection. Those who trust Christ receive holiness and perfection (sanctification) because of Christ's sinless life. Christ is both our salvation and our sanctification. In Him we are both saved and sanctified or made holy. Can you think of a greater love than this?

Because of Jesus' holy life and substitutionary death, those who believe are imputed Christ's righteousness and holiness. Our faith is credited to us as righteousness (Romans 4:3)! The righteousness that you need to enter heaven is credited to you only because you believe (have faith) in Jesus. This righteousness does not come from indulgences, good deeds or even baptism. This essential part of the true Gospel of Grace is missing in Roman Catholicism.

Holiness in Catholicism

As we have already seen, Catholicism does emphasize holiness. However, it teaches that the holiness God demands in us in order to enter heaven is *our own holiness*. This we may attain through God's grace, by our own effort, penance, prayer, and eventually through the torments and sufferings of purgatory. In purgatory, souls that are saved through faith, the sacraments, and good works are purified or made totally holy, so as to be worthy to appear in God's presence. Ultimately then, in Catholicism it is one's own personal merit and holiness which gives the right to heaven, even if the Catholic Church teaches that God's grace makes such attainment possible.

The Bible teaches that we are not saved by our own righteousness, but by the righteousness of Jesus Christ that is imputed to us when we believe (Romans 4:3). Rome, in condemning Luther, also condemned the doctrine of imputed righteousness and holiness.

The Roman Catholic Church teaches "infused" rather than imputed (credited) righteousness. Infused righteousness is the enabling of those who believe to attain salvation and sanctification through faith, sacraments, holy living, sufferings, and penance in this world, and for most, numerous years of suffering in purgatory, unless shortened by means of indulgences.

> [3]*"Abraham believed God, and it was credited [imputed] to him as righteousness."* [4]*Now when a man works, his wages are not credited to him as a gift, but as an obligation.* [5]*However, to the man who does not work but trusts God who justifies the wicked, his faith is credited as righteousness.* [6]*David says the same thing when he speaks of the blessedness of the man to whom God credits righteousness apart from works:* [7]*"Blessed are they whose transgressions are forgiven, whose sins are covered.* [8]*Blessed is the man whose sin the Lord will never count against him"* (Romans 4:3-8).

♦ According to verse three quoted above, are we saved by
our own works of righteousness, or does God impute
righteousness when we believe?

♦ According to verse six, are we made righteous by our good
works (infused righteousness), or are we made righteous
apart from works (imputed righteousness)?

♦ According to verses 6-8, what is the relationship between
God's forgiveness and man's righteousness?

> *8For it is by grace you have been saved, through faith
> —and this not from yourselves, it is the gift of God—
> 9not by works, so that no one can boast (Ephesians 2:8,
> 9).*

♦ What similarities do you find between the passage quoted
above from Ephesians and the passage from Romans
chapter four? Check the statements below that are true.

_____ They both teach that salvation is a gift of God's
grace.

_____ They both teach that salvation comes through faith
in Christ.

_____ They both teach that we are not made righteous
by works of righteousness.

_____ They both teach imputed righteousness, not
infused righteousness.

Holiness in the Bible

The word *holy* in the Bible primarily means *"set apart."* Those who believe in Jesus are set apart to God. Those who are set apart in this way are called "saints" (holy ones). All true Christians, those who have been born again by God's grace through faith in Christ, are saints (Ephesians 1:1; Philippians 1:1; Colossians 1:2; 1 Corinthians 1:2; 2 Corinthians 1:1; 1 Peter 1:2)! Believers are saints, not because of the many righteous things they have done, but because they have been made holy before God through faith in Christ (Titus 3:5; Hebrews 10:10). This holiness that is received as a gift is a "positional holiness." We are positioned before God as holy because the holiness of Christ was imputed to us when we believed, making us acceptable to God, and fulfilling in us the requirement and command to be "perfect as our heavenly Father is perfect."

Although true believers are positionally holy, they still have the duty to strive for moral or "ethical" holiness. "Ethical holiness" is attained through obedience in gratefulness to God for making us positionally holy in Christ! The Bible refers to "ethical holiness" as sanctification, perfection, or maturity (Philippians 3:16). Human experience shows that we cannot fully attain such holiness in this life, but by God's grace, through the work of the Holy Spirit in us, and through our daily effort, we are more and more conformed to the likeness of Christ. This conformity to the likeness of Christ for which we strive is the purpose for which God has called us (Romans 8:29).

Have you been made "positionally" holy? How do you know?

As one who is positionally holy, what are you doing to become ethically holy?

Holiness and the Gifts of the Spirit

The Scriptures teach that when a person is saved, the Holy Spirit bestows one or more gifts upon him (1 Corinthians 12:1). Such spiritual gifts do not, by themselves, contribute to our holiness. Gifts are granted to individual believers on behalf of the Body of Christ, the Church. They are meant for service or ministry in the Church, so that the body may function well in all aspects. God's Word warns us against pride when dealing with the gifts of the Spirit.

Spiritual gifts do not determine a believer's character, but rather his/her place of service. Being a pastor or counselor does not make one holier than a helper or giver! The recognition and exercise of one's gift is vital for the life and growth of the Church, not for one's own spiritual growth or sanctification, although this may become easier when one is exercising his or her spiritual gift.

Holiness and the Fruit of the Spirit

We read in Galatians about the fruit of the Spirit: Unlike the gifts of the Spirit, the fruit of the Spirit *is directly* related to moral or ethical holiness! Growth in holiness or Christian maturity is tantamount to evidencing the fruit or fruits of the Spirit in one's daily life.

> But the fruit of the spirit is love, joy, peace, patience, kindness, goodness, faithfulness, gentleness and self-control . . . (Galatians 5:22).

The fruit of the spirit is . . . love. All the commandments of God are summed up in this one rule: "Love your neighbor as yourself." Love is the fulfillment of the Law (Romans 13:9, 10). In the same way, all the other fruits of the Spirit (joy, peace, patience, kindness, goodness, faithfulness, gentleness and self-control) are either expressions or consequences of love.

In the middle of a long discourse on spiritual gifts (1 Corinthians 12-14), Paul makes his readers pause to meditate on the supreme importance of love (1 Corinthians 13). He begins by reminding them that the gifts of the Spirit apart from the fruit of the Spirit (love) are utterly useless, however great these may be (1 Corinthians 13:1-3)! He then describes true love. If we read his words attentively, we will discover the fruit of the Spirit there as in Galatians 5:22. He says that love is patient (patience), kind (kindness), is not proud (humility), is not rude (gentleness), is not easily angered (self-control), rejoices with the truth (joy), takes no delight in evil (goodness), always trusts (faithfulness). He concludes the chapter by saying that while the gifts will all cease, love will remain and endure forever.

Holiness and Love

Love is the fulfillment of the Law. Holiness is perfect obedience to the Law. Therefore, holiness must be related to love. To grow in holiness, we must learn to live in love.

THREE KINDS OF LOVE

In almost all modern languages people constantly use, over-use, misuse, and abuse the word LOVE. Greek, the language in which the New Testament was originally written, has three different words for love with completely different and definite meanings.

Eros, or sexual love

EROS (Ερος), from which we derive the word erotic, refers exclusively to physical or sexual love. This kind of love, which is good and holy in God's sight, finds its lawful expression only in married life. To give in and fully express it in any other way, be it premarital or extramarital, is a terrible sin in God's eyes. First Corinthians chapter seven clearly teaches about the nature of this love and its expressions.

EROS-LOVE is the basis of marriage, both as contract and commitment. This love, which probably entails the strongest emotional involvement and pleasure, is physical and emotional. According to God's Word, Eros-love is *exclusive*, shared only with one's legitimate spouse. Many of the ills of contemporary society come from a misunderstanding of God's design for this kind of love. Sexual love must not be expressed and fulfilled before or outside of marriage! To do so is either adultery or fornication, and no one who practices such sins can have a part in God's kingdom (Galatians 5:19-21).

Philia, or friendship love

PHILIA-LOVE (from Øιλος, "friend") is emotional/spiritual by its very nature, but not physical. It corresponds to our concept of true friendship. It is not exclusively limited to one person, but it is *limited to few*. Although we Christians are supposed to be friendly to all, not all people are our friends. True friends, with whom we can share our secrets, joys and problems, are generally few in number. The Bible records the friendships between David and Jonathan, and between Jesus and His three closest disciples—Peter, James and John.

Both Biblically and experientially philia-friendship takes place between people of the same sex. Because of the nature of man and woman, this kind of love generally should not be shared between persons of the opposite sex unless such friendship is intended to lead to marriage.[1]

Agape Love

By contrast to EROS and PHILIA, which are physical or emotional, AGAPE-LOVE (Αγαπη), the fruit of the Holy Spirit, is primarily an activity of the spirit, mind, and will. It does not give any physical pleasure. In fact, it generally brings suffering and self-denial. It does, however, give true spiritual

---

[1]The so-called platonic love is a true deception.

fulfillment and joy. While EROS and PHILIA are *exclusive* to one or a few, AGAPE-LOVE is *inclusive* of all. We are to love everyone with this kind of love, even our enemies (Deuteronomy 6:5; Matthew 5:43-44).

THREE KINDS OF LOVE

Eros	Philia	Agape
Physical-emotional	Emotional-spiritual	Spiritual-volitional
Exclusive to one	Limited to few	Inclusive of all
Gives intense pleasure and emotional fulfillment	Gives emotional fulfillment and joy	Gives joy and spiritual fulfillment
Holiness requires self-control	Holiness requires loyalty	Holiness requires self-sacrifice and self-denial

God is AGAPE-LOVE (1 John 4:16). He loves us with AGAPE-LOVE. He commands us to love others with AGAPE-LOVE (John 13:34; Matthew 22:36, 37). It is this kind of love that is the fruit of the Spirit of God (Galatians 5:22).

Holiness and Agape-Love

God is AGAPE-LOVE. AGAPE-LOVE is the highest form of love. It is this kind of love that God commands. It is this kind of love that should characterize our relationship to God and our fellow man. *For believers, even EROS-LOVE with one's spouse and PHILIA-LOVE with friends must include AGAPE-LOVE to be meaningful and fulfilling.*

Since God is love, we must learn how to love from Him. John 3:16 describes God's love in action:

> *For God so loved the world that he gave his one and only son, that whoever believes in Him shall not perish but have eternal life (John 3:16).*

The following principles are gleaned from this oft-quoted verse:

God loved *the world,* even though the world, in God's eyes, was not at all lovable![2] True love extends to all people, lovable or not.

God *gave*: To love is to give, not to get.

God gave *His one and only son,* the best and all He had. To love is to give one's best, one's utmost.

God gave His son, that *whoever believes*: True love is not imposing; it allows free acceptance.

God gave His Son, that whoever believes *will have eternal life.* True love aims at the ultimate good of the person beloved.

Christ's love for the Church caused Him to give Himself up for her (Ephesians 5:25). To love is to give up much of ourselves, at times our very self! Jesus taught us this with His example on the cross, but also in words:

> *Greater love has no one than this, that he lay down his life for his friends (John 15:13).*

God *commands* us to love with the same giving, self-sacrificing love with which He loves us. He expects us to give up our rights and privileges for the sake of others, even as He gave Himself up for us.

> *My command is this: Love each other as I have loved you (John 15:12).*

As we learn to love in this way, we will become more and more like our Father in heaven. We cannot be holy as He is holy until we love as He loves. To grow in holiness means to grow in AGAPE-LOVE.

---

[2]Read Romans 1:18-32 to see how God sees the sinful world.

I will become more and more like my Father in heaven only as I learn to love the way He loves.

Holiness and Human Effort

The Bible often refers to the believer's progress toward ethical holiness as *sanctification*. Unlike salvation which takes place instantly, the moment a person repents and trusts Christ, sanctification is a process.

Sanctification is first and foremost the work of the Spirit. However, the Holy Spirit only does His work when the believer cooperates in faith and strives daily to express agape-love in all its aspects (Galatians 3:1-2; 2 Peter 1:5-7).

Undoubtedly the Holy Spirit always does His work, unless prevented by the believer through voluntary sin. If a believer does not grow in holiness, it is not the Holy Spirit's fault, but his own failure to exert daily effort in obeying the Word of God. At the same time, if by God's grace he truly grows in holiness, he can never boast, because without the work of the Spirit, his effort would be futile!

Spiritual growth is much like farming. God gives rain and sunshine, without which seeds will not grow. Yet, if the farmer is lazy and fails to sow and water when needed, there will be no harvest. When the harvest is plentiful, he cannot boast, because it was God who made it grow. Without rain and sunshine, the farmer's planting and watering would be useless.

Holiness Short-Circuited

Salvation by faith plus works is a terrible heresy! We saw that in the chapters on salvation. But probably equally terrible, if not worse, is the heresy of easy-believism. This is the doctrine held by some so-called Christians, who believe that once you are saved, you can do anything you want! One is FREE! Unfortunately such people interpret freedom as freedom *to sin* instead of freedom *from sin*, as the Bible teaches. Such doctrine is not only a heresy, but a blasphemy! Paul strongly warns Christians against such interpretation of Christian freedom:

> [1]*What shall we say, then? Shall we go on sinning so that grace may increase?* [2]*By no means! [or God forbid!] We died to sin; how can we live in it any longer (Romans 6:1, 2)?*

The Bible teaches that some degree of holiness or growth toward spiritual maturity *needs* to be present as *evidence* of genuine salvation. Those who have been truly born-again will grow, though not all will grow in the same way, or at the same rate of speed. Only God sees the heart of a person. We are not to sit in judgment of those who profess faith in Christ, but we must keep in mind the clear teaching of Scripture: that no one who is truly born again goes on habitually in a lifestyle of sin.

> *No one who is born of God will continue to sin, because God's seed remains in him; he cannot go on sinning, because he has been born of God (1 John 3:9).*

As believers we should never undermine or water down with strange interpretations the clear teaching of God's Word in both Galatians and 1 John:

> [19]*The acts of sinful nature are obvious: sexual immorality, impurity and debauchery;* [20]*idolatry and witchcraft; hatred, discord, jealousy, fits of rage, selfish ambition, dissensions, factions* [21]*and envy; drunkenness, orgies and the like. I warn you, as I did before, that those who live [or go on living] like this will not inherit the kingdom of God (Galatians 5:19-21).*

> *No one who lives in Him [Christ] keeps on sinning. No one who continues to sin has either seen Him or known Him (1 John 3:6).*

The Word of God does not teach that a growing believer will never fall into sin! As a matter of fact in his first letter the apostle John states:

> ¹*My dear children, I write this to you so that you will not sin. But if anybody does sin, we have one who speaks to the Father in our defense—Jesus Christ, the Righteous One. ²He is the atoning sacrifice for our sins, and not only for ours but also for the sins of the whole world (1 John 2:1-2).*

The tense of the verb in 1 John 2 ("if anybody *does sin*") indicates the possibility of an occasional fall and could be translated "But should anyone fall into sin."[3] The tense of the verb in 1 John 3:6 ("no one who lives in Him keeps on sinning") is altogether different and refers to the ongoing practice of sin, or living in sin habitually.[4] While believers might fall into sin, they do not go on living in it habitually.

Peter describes those who are saved but fail to grow in love as useless and fruitless in their knowledge of Christ.

---

[3]The New Testament is written in the Greek language spoken at the time of Christ. So Greek grammar is always important for the understanding of concepts. In this particular case of sin in the life of believers (the tenses used by John in the second and third chapters of his first letter, as well as the statements of Paul), we must examine the meaning of the different tenses to get the true teaching and not go astray to the left nor to the right.

The tense used by 1 John 2:1 (If any one does sin) in Greek is the Aorist subjunctive (και εαη τις αμαρτη), which represents the possibility of occasional fall! It could well be translated: "But should anyone fall into sin." The sin John writes about is the breaking of God's law, especially the decalogue. This is clear from the context.

[4]In the verses quoted from chapter 3 of the same letter, the tense used is the Present Indicative (πας ο εν αυτω μενων ουχ αμαρτανει), which stands for an ongoing practice of sin or living in sin, which greatly differs from an occasional, even deliberate, fall of which one repents, confesses, and by God's grace, recovers.

The same applies to Paul's words in Galatians quoted above. After mentioning various acts of the sinful nature, Paul adds: "Those who live like this, or go on living like this, will not inherit the kingdom of God." He does not teach that those who might occasionally fall into such acts will have no part in God's kingdom.

> *5For this very reason, **make every effort** to add to your faith goodness; and to goodness, knowledge; 6and to knowledge self-control; and to self-control, perseverance; and to perseverance, godliness; 7and to godliness, brotherly kindness; and to brotherly kindness, love. 8For if you possess these qualities in increasing measure, they will keep you from being ineffective and unproductive in your knowledge of the Lord Jesus Christ (2 Peter 1:5-8).*

These verses also show that it is the believer's duty to make effort daily to grow. The Christian life is not effortless. Many in the Church have been taught to "Let go and let God." We must "let God," but we must never "let go."

Conclusion

♦ What standard does God require of those who will live in His presence (Hebrews 12:14) (p. 68)?

♦ How is a person made holy (Hebrews 10:10) (see p. 70)?

♦ According to Acts 26:18, how and when is a person forgiven and sanctified (see p. 70)?

♦ What kind of holiness does the Catholic Church teach (see p. 71)?

♦ What is the difference between infused holiness and imputed holiness (see pp. 71-72)?

♦ What is positional holiness and how is it attained (see p. 73)?

♦ What is ethical holiness and how is it attained (see p. 73)?

♦ Those who are positionally holy are referred to in the Bible as _____ (Ephesians 1:1; Philippians 1:1; Colossians 1:2; 1 Corinthians 1:2; 2 Corinthians 1:1; 1 Peter 1:2).

♦ Which of the following is related to our personal holiness (see p. 74)?
   ____ The fruit of the Spirit (Galatians 5:22)
   ____ The gifts of the Spirit (1 Corinthians 12-14).

♦ Spiritual gifts are given on behalf of the body of Christ for _____ or _____ in the Church (see p. 74).

♦ Holiness is tantamount to evidencing the _____ of the Spirit in our lives (see p. 74).

♦ What are the three kinds of love in the Bible (see pp. 75-77)?

♦ What kind of love is meant to be shared *only* by husband and wife (see p. 75)?

♦ What kind of love is shared only with friends (see p. 76)?

♦ What kind of love are we to have for all people, including our enemies (see p. 77)?

♦ Write an "**E**" before the statement below that describes *Eros* love, an "**A**" if it describes *Agape* love, and a "**P**" if it describes *Philia*.

_____ Exclusive to one person
_____ Inclusive of all people, including our enemies.
_____ Requires loyalty
_____ Limited to a few
_____ Requires self-sacrifice
_____ Spiritual-volitional
_____ Emotional-spiritual
_____ Gives spiritual fulfillment
_____ Gives intense pleasure
_____ Gives emotional fulfillment, but not physical
_____ Physical-emotional
_____ Describes God's love for the world

♦ How is holiness related to agape love (see p. 77)?

♦ Progress towards holiness is often referred to in the Scriptures as _____ (see p. 79)?

♦ In order for the Holy Spirit to do His work in me, I must cooperate in faith and _____ daily to express _____ in all its aspects (see p. 79).

♦   How is our growth in holiness like farming (see p. 79)?

A life of sin is an indication that a person has not been truly born-again. An occasional fall is a sign of backsliding. Sinfulness as imperfection, limitations, and weakness is present in all believers (1 John 1:8-10). Those, however, who have truly been born again are indeed growing toward holiness.

♦   Write a brief testimony telling how God has changed you from the inside out.

♦   Spend a few minutes in prayer thanking God for imputed righteousness.

Chapter 7

The Truth About The Priesthood

I was born into a very Catholic family that boasted having three priests and at least three nuns. At a very early age, I dreamed of becoming a missionary priest myself. At age 11, I entered seminary.

Soon after admission, a rector whom I loved and esteemed very much presented the priestly vocation as the noblest and most sublime on earth. *"There is no greater or nobler person on earth than the Catholic priest,"* he said! *"Only the priest can offer the sacrifice of the Mass, changing bread into the body of Christ, and wine into His blood! Mary, the mother of God, cannot do that! The angels cannot do that!"*

He continued to impress us with the loftiness of the priestly office: *"Nobody on earth, whether king or emperor, can have his sins forgiven unless he kneels in front of a priest, confesses his sins to him, and carries out the penance imposed by him!"*

These thoughts were used to inspire us throughout the fifteen long years of strict disciplinary training required of those who will become priests.

In those early years, while we still knew little or nothing about marriage, this same rector attempted to prepare us for a life of celibacy. He said: *"As Jesus never married; as the angels do not marry; as Mary, the mother of God, never lived as a wife to Joseph because of her special mission; so the priest can never have a wife, because that would defile him!"*

Our rector also promised us that if we became priests, the salvation of our relatives would be assured up to the fourth generation. He based this assurance on the teachings of St. John Bosco, founder of the Salesian religious society.

Priests in Old Testament Israel

There are three priesthoods in the Old Testament: The Aaronic priesthood, from Aaron, Moses' brother;[1] the levitical priesthood, for the men of Levi's tribe;[2] and the special priesthood of Melchizedek, king of Salem.[3]

The Old Testament priests had specific and exclusive tasks ranging from care of the temple to offering of sacrifices and pronouncement of forgiveness for sins. They were set apart by God as mediators between God and man. The priesthoods of the Old Testament reveal that God did not deal directly with sinful people, but through priests set apart for this purpose. These earthly priesthoods, however, were inadequate and temporary. The sacrifices these priests offered could not take away sin.

> [1]*The law* [including priests and sacrifices] *is only a shadow of the good things that are coming—not the realities themselves. For this reason it can never, by the same sacrifices repeated endlessly year after year, make perfect those who draw near to worship. ²If it could, would they*

---

[1]Exodus 28:1; Numbers 17; Hebrews 5:1-7.
[2]Numbers 1:53; 8:6; 2 Chronicles 31:2; Hebrews 7:11.
[3]Genesis 14:18; Psalm 110:4; Hebrews 7:11.

not have stopped being offered? For the worshipers would have been cleansed once for all, and would no longer have felt guilty for their sins. ³But those sacrifices are an annual reminder of sins, ⁴because it is impossible for the blood of bulls and goats to take away sins (Hebrews 10:1-4).

Through these priests God revealed and visualized man's need for both a mediator and a sacrifice for sin. They pictured what was needed but were inadequate to satisfy the need. Jesus, however, the eternal Son of God, was able to satisfy that need. He was set apart by the Father in eternity past to be our priest, the one mediator between God and man who would offer once for all the only acceptable sacrifice for sin.

¹¹Day after day every [Old Testament] priest stands and performs his religious duties; again and again he offers the same sacrifices, which can never take away sins. ¹²But when this priest [Christ] had offered for all time one sacrifice for sins, he sat down at the right hand of God . . . . ¹⁴because by one sacrifice he has made perfect forever those who are being made holy (Hebrews 10:11-14).

Christ the Great High Priest

What the priests of the Old Testament did in an earthly tabernacle, Christ has done in the heavenly one. The work of the Old Testament priest was but a finite, earthly representation of the eternal, all-sufficient work of Christ.

¹¹When Christ came as high priest . . . he went through the greater and more perfect tabernacle that is not man-made, that is to say, not a part of this creation. ¹²He did not enter by means of the blood of goats and calves, but he entered the Most Holy Place once for all by his own

> *blood, having obtained eternal redemption . . . [26]he has appeared once for all at the end of the ages to do away with sin by the sacrifice of himself (Hebrews 9:11-12, 26).*

Christ, our great high priest, offered Himself as the lamb of God who takes away the sins of the world. There is no other sacrifice for sins (Hebrews 10:18). There is no other priest.

If the only sacrifice for sins has already been offered once and for all by the great heavenly High Priest, what need is there now for an earthly priesthood to continue offering sacrifices for the forgiveness of sins?

No Priests in the New Testament Church

The Greek word for priest in both Old and New Testaments is *hiereus*[4], which means sacred or consecrated person, set apart for God's service. This term must not be confused with the word *presbyteros*,[5] which means elder or older man, senior people to whom leadership was entrusted. The apostle Peter, an apostle and a church leader, spoke of himself as a "fellow elder" (*presbyteros*), but never as a priest (1 Peter 5:1).

Edward was a Roman Catholic priest who became my friend. One day, he tried to prove to me that there was a New Testament priesthood, just as there was in the Old Testament. I answered him: "Edward, I challenge you to find a single verse, anywhere in the New Testament, where the word 'priest' [*hiereus*] is attributed to any one person, whether apostle or disciple or any believer in particular." He had taken for granted that the apostles had been ordained priests and consecrated bishops by Jesus in the upper room the night of the last supper, as he had been taught in theology classes. He was surprised to discover that there was no reference in the Bible to a New Testament priesthood.

---

[4]ἱερεύς, Priest.
[5]πρεσβυτερος, Elder.

A Kingdom of Priests

You will not find a group of men in the New Testament Church who have been chosen by God to lead the Church and given the privileges and powers of mediation. In the New Testament Church there is just one high priest and only one mediator between God and man.

> *⁵For there is one God, and one mediator between God and men, the man Christ Jesus, ⁶who gave himself as a ransom for all men (1 Timothy 2:5, 6).*

What you will find in the New Testament is that all believers are priests, and the Church itself is a royal priesthood. We are priests, not in the sense that we offer sacrifices for our own sins and for the sins of others, but in the sense that we all have direct access to the Father by the way opened to us through Christ's sacrifice.

> *¹⁹Therefore, brothers, since we have confidence to enter the Most Holy Place by the blood of Jesus, ²⁰by a new and living way opened for us through the curtain, that is, his body, ²¹and since we have a great priest over the house of God, ²²let us draw near to God with a sincere heart in full assurance of faith . . . (Hebrews 10:19-22).*

Since direct access to God is a priestly prerogative, it follows that in the New Testament ALL TRUE BELIEVERS ARE PRIESTS. This truth is clearly taught in the Scriptures.

> *⁴As you come to him, the living Stone—rejected by men but chosen by God and precious to him—⁵you also, like living stones, are being built into a spiritual house to be a <u>holy priesthood</u>, offering spiritual sacrifices acceptable to God through Jesus Christ (1 Peter 2:4-5).*

> *But you are a chosen people, a <u>royal priesthood</u>, a holy nation, a people belonging to God, that you may declare*

the praises of Him who called you out of darkness into His wonderful light (1 Peter 2:9).

These words were not written to a select group of men who were set apart to be church leaders, but to ordinary believers scattered throughout different parts of the Roman empire (1 Peter 1:1-2). Every believer is a priest! Together they are a kingdom of priests:

> *⁵. . . To him who loves us and has freed us from our sins by His blood, ⁶and has made us to be a <u>kingdom of priests</u> to serve His God and Father—to Him be glory and power for ever and ever. Amen (Revelation 1:5b-6).*

Children of God Need no Priests

The Scriptures teach that those who are born again through faith in the Lord Jesus are children of God.

> *Yet to all who received him, to those who believed in his name, he gave the right to become children of God (John 1:12).*

God was a Father to His people in the Old Testament. He loved them and showed them mercy as a Father would. However, people then did not address him as Father in prayer. Jesus, however, prayed to His Father (Luke 23:34; Matthew 11:25; John 17:1, 11, 24, 25), and it was He who taught us to pray in that way:

> *This, then, is how you should pray: "Our Father in heaven . . ." (Matthew 6:9).*

Jesus brings believers into a new relationship with God. In Christ, we are children of God. Children do not need mediators to have recourse to their fathers! They have direct access. The Scriptures clearly teach that in Jesus we have such access to our Father in heaven:

> *For through Him we both* [Jews and Gentiles] *have access to the Father in one Spirit (Ephesians 2:18).*

> [1] *... through our Lord Jesus Christ,* [2]*through whom we have gained access by faith into His grace in which we now stand (Romans 5:1-2).*

Why No More Special Priesthood in the New Testament?

The unique function of the Old Testament priesthood, aside from the care of the temple, was the offering of sacrifices and the pronouncement of forgiveness. No one, not even kings, could usurp this power and function of the priest. Roman Catholicism, Greek Orthodox religion, and even some mainline Protestant denominations, try to maintain a special priesthood because they believe that in the "holy mass" we still have a sacrifice to offer for the forgiveness of sins, and that someone must have the authority either to forgive sins or to pronounce forgiveness! We will see the teaching of God's Word concerning the so-called "sacrifice of the mass." In that same chapter we will also consider whether the Bible teaches that someone should be endowed with the power to forgive sins!

The Blunder of History and Religion

The tragic mistake of Catholicism with regard to church leadership is that they have made their church leaders into priests and taken the God-given privileges of priesthood away from the believer. The Catholic priest still stands between God and His people whom He reconciled. The veil in the temple that God tore from top to bottom when Jesus died on the cross, the Catholic Church has repaired and replaced.

The Church of Rome has complicated the structure of church leadership tremendously. A hierarchy (a sacred or sacramental chain of command) has been developed. At the top of this sacred chain is the Pope; he is the head of the Church, and all bishops, priests and lay persons are under him. Then there is the bishop, the head of a diocese. Under him are all his parish priests, under whom are the parishioners.

What does the Bible teach? First of all there is no Pope. Only Christ is the head of the Church (Ephesians 5:23). Then we have three different words for church leaders, besides the deacons, who are supposed to assist the

THE CATHOLIC CHURCH

The Teaching Church

The Pope: Head of the Church

↓

The Bishops: Heads of Dioceses

↓

The Priests: Heads of Parishes

↓

The Learning Church
The Laity

The New Testament Church

Christ the Head of the Church

↓

Undershepherds (pastor, elders, overseers)

equipping believers

to do works of service

leaders in the government of the Church. These words are: bishop or overseer (*episcopos*), elder (*presbyteros*) and pastor (*poimen*). An attentive study of God's Word will clearly show that these words do not refer to three different persons, but to different tasks and aspects of the same office.

The apostle Paul in his farewell speech to the **elders** of Ephesus said:

> Keep watch over yourselves and all the flock of which the Holy Spirit has made you **overseers** [bishops]. Be **shepherds** [pastors] of the church of God, which he bought with his own blood (Acts 20:28).

The apostle Peter uses a very similar expression in his first letter:

> [1]To the elders among you, I appeal as a fellow elder, a witness of Christ's sufferings and one who also will share in the glory to be revealed: [2]Be shepherds of God's flock that is under your care, serving as overseers [bishops]— not because you must, but because you are willing, as God wants you to be; not greedy for money, but eager to serve; [3]not lording it over those entrusted to you, but being examples to the flock (1 Peter 5:1-3).

From these passages, as well as from the rest of the New Testament writings, we see that the church leaders are called by these three different names to show different aspects of the same office. Elder (*presbyteros*) refers to the physical and spiritual maturity of the leader. Pastor (shepherd) refers to his main task to spiritually feed the flock. Bishop or overseer (*episcopos*) refers to his main office of overseeing the church ministry, by training the believers for different kinds of service:

> [11]It was he who gave some to be . . . pastors and teachers, [12]to prepare God's people for works of service . . . (Ephesians 4:11-12).

Conclusion

God has given the Church leaders, not to stand in the place of Jesus and mediate, but to serve by equipping and nurturing God's flock. Christ is the sole head of the Church, and the only mediator between God and man.

♦ What are three tasks of the Old Testament priest (see p. 87)?

_____ The care of the _____

_____ The offering of _____

_____ The pronouncement of _____ of _____

♦ What kind of sacrifices did the Old Testament priests offer (Hebrews 10:1-4) (see p. 88)?

_____ Money

_____ Fruits and vegetables

_____ The blood of bulls and goats

♦ Mark the statements below that are *true* with a "T", and those that are *false* with an "F".

_____ The blood of bulls and goats took away sin.

_____ The sacrifices that these priests offered were the real thing.

_____ The sacrifices that these Old Testament priests offered did make people perfect forever.

_____ The sacrifices that these priests offered could not make a person perfect forever.

_____ The blood of bulls and goats could not take away sin.

_____ The sacrifices that these priests offered were just shadows of the real sacrifice of Jesus that does take away sin and makes people perfect forever.

♦ What sacrifice did Jesus offer for sin (see pp. 88-89; Hebrews 9:11-12, 26)?

♦ Where did Jesus offer this sacrifice (see pp. 88-89; Hebrews 9:11-12, 26)?

♦ How many times was this sacrifice offered (see p. 89; Hebrews 9:11-12, 26)?

♦ What sacrifice other than the sacrifice of Jesus can be offered for sins (Hebrews 10:18) (see p. 89)?

♦ Why do you think that the church leaders in the New Testament are never referred to as priests (see p. 89)?

♦ Can you find a passage in the Bible that teaches that the apostles were ordained as priests by the Lord Jesus? If so, write the reference here (see p. 91).

♦ Can you find a passage in the Bible that teaches where a church leader is singled out as a priest? Can you find any evidence of a New Testament priesthood (see p. 91)?

♦ Who is the only mediator between God and man, the One Great Priest in the Church, the One who offered the only acceptable sacrifice for sin (see p. 90)?

♦ In what sense are all believers priests? Choose the one correct answer below (see pp. 91-92):

     ____ We are all priests because we all offer sacrifices for sin.

_____ We are all priests in the sense that we all have access into God's holy place by the blood of Jesus, and can offer him the sacrifices of service, thanksgiving, and praise.

♦ What is the "great blunder of history and religion" (see p. 92)?

♦ What are the three titles given to church leaders in the New Testament Church (see p. 94)?

♦ What does the title "Elder" imply about the person called to leadership in the church (see pp. 94-95)?

♦ What does the title "Pastor" denote concerning a church leader's role (see p. 94)?

♦ What does the title "Bishop" or "Overseer" convey concerning the person called to leadership in a local church (see p. 94)?

♦ Do these titles describe three different persons or three functions of the same office (see p. 94)?

♦ Write a brief paragraph expressing how this chapter has changed your view of church leaders.

Chapter 8

The Truth About Sacrifice

One morning, a few weeks before my conversion to
Christ, I was celebrating Mass as usual. As I addressed
the congregation with the words *"Brethren, pray that our sacrifice
may be acceptable to God, the Father Almighty,"* I heard, not
the people's response, "May God accept the sacrifice from your
hands . . .", but rather the words of Hebrews 10:18, *"And where
these* [sins] *have been forgiven, there is no longer any sacrifice
for sin."*

About two weeks later I met an Evangelical pastor. I sought
to convince him of the advantages of having priests and a
sacrifice for the forgiveness of sins (the mass). I was struck
by his answer. He quoted Hebrews 10:18. I knew that he was
right. His response was the Word of God, while my teaching
and belief was the doctrine of men.

The Teaching of God's Word
About the Sacrifice

> *The death he died, he died to sin **once for all**; but the life he lives, he lives to God (Romans 6:10).*

> *We have been made holy through the sacrifice of the body of Jesus Christ **once for all** (Hebrews 10:10).*

> *But when this Priest [Jesus] had offered **for all time one sacrifice for sins**, He sat down at the right hand of God (Hebrews 10:12).*

> *And where these [sins] have been forgiven, **there is no longer any sacrifice for sin** (Hebrews 10:18).*

The Doctrine of the Catholic Church
About the Mass

> *Remembering that the work of redemption is continually accomplished in the mystery of the Eucharist Sacrifice, priests are to celebrate frequently; indeed daily celebration is strongly recommended, since even if the faithful cannot be present, it is the act of Christ and the Church in which priests fulfill their principal function (Canon 904 of the revised Canon Law, 1984).*

> *The celebration of the Eucharist [Mass] is the action of Christ Himself and the Church; in it Christ the Lord, by the ministry of the priest, **offers Himself**, substantially present under the forms of bread and wine, to God the Father and **gives Himself as spiritual food** to the faithful who are associated with His offering (Canon 899, Section 1, 1984).*

> *Holy Mass is a real sacrifice instituted by Christ at the Last Supper.[1]*

---

[1]Neuner, Ross, and Rahner, S.J. *(The Teaching of the Catholic Church.)* p. 279.

According to the above quoted Canon Laws, the Mass (Eucharist) is a sacrifice. The priests are to frequently offer this sacrifice of the Mass. How does this compare to what the Bible teaches in the verses shown above?

In the twenty-second session of the Council of Trent the Pope and the bishops dealt with the so-called sacrifice of the Mass, and laid down all the dogmatic statements:

> *Inasmuch as in this divine sacrifice which is celebrated in the Mass there is contained and immolated in an unbloody manner the same Christ who once offered Himself in a bloody manner on the altar of the cross, the Holy Council [!] teaches that this [the Mass] is truly propitiatory and has this effect that if, contrite and penitent, with sincere heart and upright faith, with fear and reverence, we draw nigh to God, "we obtain mercy and find grace in seasonable aid" (Hebrews 4:16). For, appeased by this sacrifice, the Lord grants the grace and gift of penitence (repentance), and pardons even the gravest crimes and sins.*[2]

The Mass is here called an unbloody sacrifice, yet it is said to obtain forgiveness of sins. The Word of God says that *"Without the shedding of blood there is no forgiveness"* (Hebrews 9:22)! After a long explanation trying to justify masses for the living and for the dead, and the celebration in Latin only and not in spoken languages (which now the Catholic Church disregards, showing how fragile the Pope's infallibility is!), the Council boldly states:

> *If anyone will say that in the Mass a true and real sacrifice is not offered,* anathema sit *[Let him be excommunicated or condemned!].*

---

[2]Ibid., p. 296, No. 514.

If anyone will say that by the words "Do this in memory of me" Christ did not institute the Apostles Priests, let him be excommunicated.

If anyone will say that the sacrifice of the Mass is only one of praise and thanksgiving; or that it is a mere commemoration of the sacrifice consummated on the cross but not a propitiatory one [not obtaining forgiveness of sins in itself], and not to be offered for the living and for the dead, for sins, punishments, satisfactions, and other necessities, let him be excommunicated.

If anyone will say that it is an imposture to celebrate Masses in honor of the saints [canonized saints] and in order to obtain their intercession with God, as the Church intends, let him be excommunicated."[3]

Note that the Council states that a true and real sacrifice (although unbloody) is offered in the Eucharist. The Council goes on to excommunicate or condemn anyone who denies that the Mass is a true and propitiatory sacrifice.

The Contrast Between the Biblical Teaching and the Religion of Rome

The Word of God says that Jesus died only once and that there is no longer any sacrifice for sins. Rome teaches that the Mass is a mystical but real sacrifice, the continued sacrifice of Jesus on the cross.

---

[3]Ibid., p. 300, Nos. 521-523.

The Teaching of the Word of God	The Teaching of the Catholic Church
Jesus offered Himself *once for all* (Hebrews 10:10, 12).	Jesus offered Himself *continually.*
There is no longer any sacrifice for sins (Hebrews 10:18).	The Mass is a mystical but real sacrifice to be offered for sins daily.
Without the shedding of *blood* there is no forgiveness of sins (Hebrews 9:22).	The sacrifice of the Mass is an *unbloody* sacrifice offered for the forgiveness of sins.

♦   Comparing what God says in His Word about the sacrifice of Jesus with what the Catholic Church teaches through their canons, mark each of the following statements either true or false.

_____ The teaching of the Catholic Church is consistent with the teaching of God's Word.

_____ The teaching of the Catholic Church is contrary to the teaching of God's Word.

_____ Both the Catholic Church and the Bible are correct.

_____ The Bible and the Catholic Church cannot both be correct because they contradict each other.

Look carefully at the dogmatic statements of the Council beginning at the bottom of page 100. What dilemma do these statements create for the person who chooses to believe the clear teaching of God's Word but feels certain loyalties to the Catholic Church?

Jesus and the Last Supper

The supper that Jesus celebrated with his disciples in the upper room on the night that he was betrayed was a Jewish Passover meal. The elements of the meal were the same elements used by the Israelites to commemorate the time when God used His mighty power to deliver their nation from slavery in Egypt. This meal, however, was different than other Passover meals. At this Passover meal, Jesus changed the symbolism of the elements, making them a memorial to His death on the cross (His body and His blood) and our ultimate deliverance from slavery to sin and eternal death. The words "new covenant" used by the Lord Jesus on this occasion are all-important. The meal that once symbolized a covenant (agreement) that God made with the nation of Israel, would now symbolize a new covenant God has made with all who believe in Jesus.

The Old Testament events, Israel's slavery in Egypt and the miraculous deliverance, are both historical facts and prophetic symbolic events. They typified man's slavery to sin and his salvation through **Christ.**

The bread at the Passover celebration reminded the Jews of the manna their fathers ate in the desert. The wine was a symbol of the lamb's blood sprinkled over the doorposts of all Israelite homes, which kept them from losing their firstborn sons as death visited all Egyptian families.

Jesus is the true Passover lamb since through his blood we are delivered from death. He is the bread from heaven that gives life to the world. The elements of the Passover meal, symbols of an old covenant and a memorial to Israel's deliverance from slavery in Egypt, would be appropriate symbols of a new covenant—and a memorial to the believer's deliverance from slavery to sin and eternal death. In initiating the new covenant (Luke 22:20), Jesus transformed the Passover meal into the Lord's supper. He urged believers to continue celebrating a Passover meal, but with a completely new meaning: the bread now symbolizing the broken body of Jesus, and the wine His blood. The whole meal is a memorial to the death of Christ on the cross by which he offered Himself as a sacrifice for sins once and for all.

Just as the Jewish Passover meal was a memorial to certain historical events, so the Lord's supper is a memorial to the death of Christ. The Lord's supper is no more a repetition of the sacrifice of Jesus than the Passover meal was a reliving of the events of history. Both times that Jesus commanded his followers to partake of an element of the supper he said, "*Do this in remembrance of me.*" He intended the supper he instituted to be a commemoration, not a repeated sacrifice:

> [23] *For I received from the Lord what I also passed on to you: The Lord Jesus, on the night He was betrayed, took bread,* [24] *and when He had given thanks, He broke it and said: "This is my body, which is for you; do this in* **remembrance of me**." [25]*In the same way after supper He took the cup, saying, "This cup is the new covenant in my blood; do this, whenever you drink it, in* **remembrance of me**" *(1 Corinthians 11:23-25).*

To repeat the sacrifice of Jesus in the Mass would be to repeat his death. How can He die again since He is already gloriously seated at the right hand of His Father?

Think a moment what mysticism the Catholic religion has introduced. Over 300,000 priests celebrate Mass daily! On Sundays there may be over half a million Masses said all over the world! At every Mass Jesus is supposed to die again and be eaten as food by millions of Catholics! Moreover, considering that the Catholic Church teaches that the wine is the real, mystical (?) but physical blood of Jesus, try to think how much blood the body of Christ Jesus is supposed to have!

The Doctrine of Transubstantiation

According to the Catholic canons, upon pronouncement by the priest, the elements of bread and wine truly become the body and blood of Christ. This is the doctrine of transubstantiation (change of substance). There are two main passages of Scripture that the Catholic Church uses to prove this doctrine. The first is Jesus' words in the upper room: *This*

is my body (Matthew 26:26), and *This is my blood of the covenant* (Matthew 26:28).

The argument goes like this: If Jesus says that the bread and wine are his body and blood, who are we to say that He means they symbolize His body and blood? Are we not supposed to take His word literally?

It is true that we are always supposed to accept the Word of God for what it says. The Bible is written in human languages, which have a definite grammar. All languages frequently use what are called figures of speech, expressions which by their very nature are obviously figurative. For example, Jesus says in John 14:6: *I am the way* [οδος in the Greek, meaning literally *road*). Do we take His words to mean that Jesus is literally the road that goes to the Father? Obviously, Jesus was using a figure of speech. He meant that just as we need a road to any destination, through Him alone we can go to the Father. So we translate the Greek word "road" with the word "way."

The example in John 10:7 is even clearer. Jesus said: *I am the gate for the sheep.* We all understand the two figures of speech in this one sentence. Surely Jesus is no gate! We are not sheep! But it is a beautiful and powerful expression which helps us clearly understand that as the sheep must pass through the gate to find green pasture, so we must all pass through Him to go to heaven. By calling men "sheep," He also conveys His love and care for us as a shepherd for his sheep! The Bible is full of figurative expressions, which Catholics also accept.

Jesus often represented himself in a figure. He said he was the light, the gate, the good shepherd, the road, the true vine. He did not mean that he was a candle, or a gate, or a bush. He was speaking figuratively. He did that frequently. It should not surprise us that He would use figures of bread and wine in the same way.

Luke and Paul quote Jesus as saying: *This cup is the New Covenant in my blood* (Luke 22:20; 1 Corinthians 11:25). They

do not follow Matthew's quote: *This is my blood* (Matthew 26:28). (Jesus said it both ways. Matthew quoted the shorter phrase, Paul and Luke the longer. The longer is an interpretation of the shorter). Paul and Luke definitely understood Jesus to be speaking figuratively.

The most natural interpretation of Jesus' words is "This represents my body." If someone holds up a picture, points to it, and says "This is me," the people around him will understand what he is saying. They would not suppose that he meant, "This picture actually is my body. My body and blood are really present under the appearance of ink and paper." In fact, they would not even entertain such an absurdity unless the one holding the picture explained himself to them. There is no record of any such explanation by the Lord Jesus. He simply held up the bread and said, *This is my body.* That was all that was needed. The disciples understood what he meant.

♦ Read Matthew 26:29. How did Jesus refer to the contents of the cup after the pronouncement?

Jesus referred to the wine as "fruit of the vine" after the words of consecration were spoken and the transformation supposedly took place (Matthew 26:29). It was wine before the pronouncement. It was still wine afterward.

Suppose for the sake of argument that Jesus literally meant the bread he was holding in his hands was his own flesh and blood. He did not say to the apostles, "I will place my body into your hands every time you speak the words of consecration." No such explanation was ever given, though it would certainly have been necessary if the disciples were to understand him. The whole idea is foreign to the teaching of Jesus as recorded by the apostles in the Scripture.

We can take this argument one step further. Suppose Jesus gave the apostles authority to speak "the words of consecration" and change the elements of bread and wine into the body and blood of Jesus. Still, he did not give them permission to pass

that authority on to someone else. There is no record of any such apostolic succession.

The second passage of Scripture the Roman Catholic Church uses in trying to defend the doctrine of transubstantiation is John 6:53-55:

> [53] . . . *I tell you the truth, unless you eat the flesh of the Son of Man and drink His blood, you have no life in you.* [54]*Whoever eats my flesh and drinks my blood has eternal life, and I will raise him up at the last day.* [55]*For my flesh is real food and my blood is real drink.*

Catholics take it for granted that these words of Jesus were uttered in connection with the last supper. This is **not** the case! The context of John 6:50,51 is the feeding of the 5,000 on the shore of the Sea of Galilee during Jesus' public ministry, long before the experiences in the upper room. His audience on the shores of the Sea of Galilee was mostly unbelieving Jews. In the upper room, he was speaking to his beloved disciples. The disciples could not have understood these verses as instruction concerning the ordinance of holy communion since the "sacrament"[4] had not yet been instituted, and would not be instituted until the gathering in the upper room two years later.

Jesus had just fed five thousand people with a few loaves of bread. This miracle, which demonstrated that Jesus was the prophet "like Moses," prophesied about in the Old Testament, gave Jesus an opportunity to illustrate a great truth concerning Himself. He compares Himself to the manna that fell from heaven in the wilderness, giving life to the wandering Jews. He claimed He is the true bread from heaven who gives life

---

[4]Theologically the word "sacrament" when used to refer to baptism and the Lord's supper is acceptable, since *sacermentum* means *sacred thing or action.* Yet we would rather avoid its use, since in Catholic Theology a *sacrament* is *an effective sign of grace which truly confers what it symbolizes.* Carefully considered, this definition is a contradiction.

to the world. In the process He urged His hearers to believe in Him.

> *35 . . . I am the bread of life . . . 36But as I told you, you have seen me and still you do not **believe** . . . 40For my Father's will is that everyone who looks to the Son and **believes** in Him shall have eternal life . . . 47I tell you the truth, He who **believes** has everlasting life. 48I am the bread of life. 51 . . . If anyone eats of this bread, he will live forever. This bread is my flesh, which I will give for the life of the world (John 6:35-36, 40, 47-48, 51).*

The context teaches that we eat the true bread from heaven, not by participation in a sacrament, but by believing in Jesus. Jesus used other such figures in his public teaching to illustrate faith in Him. He spoke of "drinking living water" (John 4:13,14); of "coming to the light" (John 3:20); of "hearing the shepherd's voice" (John 10:4-6); and of "eating bread from heaven" (John 6:51). Each of these figures of speech was intended to teach faith (Cp. John 6:35, 36, 40, 46). John chapter six can no more be used to prove that bread on the communion table is the literal body of Jesus than John chapter four can be used to prove that the Holy Spirit is water drunk from a well!

Eating bread (the main staple in the Middle East) is necessary for physical life. In the same way, faith in Christ is necessary for eternal life. Truly Jesus is the bread from heaven for our spiritual life. Jesus was not making cannibals of his followers by commanding them to literally eat His flesh and drink His blood. Far from it, Jesus used such vivid language to convey two most important spiritual truths: (1) the necessity of His death by the shedding of blood and (2) our need to receive Jesus by faith. Jesus Himself, to prevent a too-literal interpretation, concluded the conversation by saying:

> *61 . . . Does this offend you? . . . 63The Spirit gives life, the flesh counts for nothing. The words I have spoken to you*

are spirit and they are life. [64] Yet there are some of you who do not believe (John 6:61-64).

Conclusion

♦ How many times did Jesus die for sins according to Romans 6:10 (see p. 99)?

♦ How many times will Jesus be sacrificed for sins according to Hebrews 10:10 (see p. 99)?

♦ Why do you think Jesus "sat down" after he offered once for all time the only sacrifice for sins (see p. 99)?
____ He sat down because His work was finished, and no other sacrifices needed to be offered.
____ He sat down to rest because he was tired.
____ Other:

♦ According to Hebrews 10, our sins are forgiven through the sacrifice of Christ, and once our sins are forgiven, "there is ___ _____ any sacrifice for sins" (Hebrews 10:18) (see p. 99).

In your opinion, considering all that the Bible says about the Lord's Supper, can a believer still accept the Catholic Mass as a good way of worshiping God?

♦ What is the Mass (Eucharist) according to Canon Laws quoted on pages 99-102?

♦ According to the laws of the Church, how often should the priest offer the sacrifice of the Mass (see p. 100)?

♦ According to the Council of Trent, what kind of sacrifice is offered in the Eucharist? Check the two correct answers (see p. 101).

    ____ Only a commemoration of the sacrifice of Christ.

    ____ A propitiatory sacrifice that obtains forgiveness of sins.

    ____ A true and real sacrifice (although unbloody) of the body and blood of Christ.

♦ What does the Council of Trent pronounce concerning the person who denies that the Mass is a true and propitiatory sacrifice (see p. 101)?

♦ Imagine that you are one of the Reformers, a Catholic who wishes to be loyal to the Church, but because of your study of Scripture you are aware that there are contradictions between what your Church teaches and what the early apostles taught in the Word of God. What will you do?

    ____ I would choose to believe the Scriptures (The Apostles' teaching).

    ____ I would go on believing the Church and ignore what the Bible says.

♦ If you chose to believe the Bible, what would be your course of action?

    ____ I would keep quiet about what I knew so as not to cause trouble. Doctrine is not that important anyway.

    ____ I would seek to reform the Church by clearly explaining to anyone who would listen what the Word of God says.

♦   What event in the history of Israel did the Passover meal commemorate?

♦   What did the bread and the wine symbolize in the Passover meal?

♦   How did Jesus change the symbolism of the Passover meal? What do the bread and the wine now represent?

♦   In what way is Jesus the true Passover lamb?

♦   How many times did Jesus command his disciples to celebrate the Lord's Supper "in remembrance" of Him?

♦   Do you think that Jesus intended the Lord's Supper to be a memorial? Why or why not?

♦   Read John 8:12. What did Jesus call himself in this verse?

♦   Read John 10:11. How does Jesus refer to himself in this verse?

♦   Read John 15:1. What does Jesus say about himself in this verse?

♦ According to Luke 22:20, what did Jesus say about the cup?

♦ According to 1 Corinthians 11:25, what did Jesus say about the cup?

♦ How did Jesus refer to the wine after the words of pronouncement in the upper room (Matthew 26:29)?

♦ What do you think is the most logical explanation of the simple words of Jesus, "This is my body"?

    ____ He meant that the bread was literally his body. He meant that every time one of the apostles said those words at a supper such as this the bread they held in their hand would also become His body. His words imply that all successors of the Apostles will have the same power to change the bread into the body of Jesus.

    ____ He meant "This bread represents my body."

♦ When and where did Jesus say: *Unless you eat the flesh of the Son of Man and drink His blood, you have no life in you?*

♦ To whom was Jesus speaking when He said these words?

♦ What did Jesus do just before saying these words?

◆ In context, what did Jesus mean when He spoke these words? Choose one.

      ____ He meant that all those who believe in Him will receive eternal life.

      ____ He meant that those who will someday eat His flesh in the sacrifice of the Mass will receive forgiveness of sins.

Chapter 9

The Truth About Celibacy

I made the vow of chastity or celibacy for the first time at age 16. I was taught that priests should lead a life totally free from any sexual sin, for they are supposed to be like Christ. Renouncing marriage is only part of the vow. The ideal is that priests should be like angels. Sins of impurity were emphasized so much that all other sins seemed small or venial. Our spiritual director once told us: "Sexual impurity is practically the only mortal sin a seminarian or priest is able to commit. All other sins are a trifle compared to this! Here is where Satan will have priests and religious fall!"

At age 26, I was ordained a priest. I was so strict with myself that I didn't even dare look a girl in the eyes when talking to her. I would never sit next to a woman in cars or public vehicles, strictly following the advice of the founder of our order. It was only God, in His love and mercy, who kept me from any moral fall in this area. Still, having been so careful myself, I was scandalized when I came to know of the horrible sexual sins committed by many priests and bishops!

I know, personally, many priests who would have avoided so many sexual sins if only they were allowed to marry. These were noble-minded people who had left the world to serve God and to devote themselves to the things of the Spirit. Sins of fornication, adultery, homosexuality or pedophilia could have been avoided by a healthy marriage! But a compulsory celibacy, even if with a noble pretext, caused them to fall.

When I became a Christian and began to feel free to read "non-Catholic" literature, I saw my ideas confirmed by the facts! Contemporary surveys show now more than ever that many Roman Catholic priests, bishops, and religious in seminaries, convents and parishes are both victims themselves of sexual sins, and make victims of others.

I know of scores of unhappy women who have children, but *officially* have no husband. They are confined to stay *at home*, unable to lead a normal life, or to introduce their "husbands" to others! They, too, are victims of the priests' vow of celibacy.

Can the *vow of celibacy* possibly be from God when it is a direct occasion of sin? So much pain and heartache, and so many sins, could be avoided if only the Catholic Church held on to what God's Word says—that a pastor or bishop should be a faithful husband (1 Timothy 3:2).

Celibacy and Priesthood

The Roman Catholic Church officially imposed celibacy on all priests in the eleventh century (AD 1079). Although many monastics practiced celibacy prior to that time, there was no law forbidding the clergy to be married. Several Popes, many bishops, and very many priests were married men.

I was taught in the seminary that several things contributed to the decision to forbid the clergy to marry: rampant immorality in Catholic families; married priests breaking the 'seal of secrecy' by telling their wives what they had heard in the confessional;

and fear of losing church property to the children of priests. But, the greatest reason for the decision was a Gnostic philosophy embraced by theologians in the Middle Ages which taught that "the soul is basically good, while the flesh is fundamentally evil." This *false* assumption led to the conviction that sexual activity was a "necessary *evil* for the propagation of mankind." Since sexual activity is substantially evil, those who have been called to serve God as "His priests," to be endowed with great supernatural powers, should not be entangled with it.

Variations of Gnostic teaching have been around for a long time. The apostle John wrote against such doctrines in the first century. There were some way back then who taught that since matter is evil, Christ could not have come in the flesh. John answered such false prophets by testifying that he had seen the body of the Lord with his eyes and touched it with his hands (1 John 1:1-3). He warned the early church:

> *[2]This is how you can recognize the Spirit of God: Every spirit that acknowledges that Jesus Christ has come in the flesh is from God, [3]but every spirit that does not acknowledge Jesus is not from God. This is the spirit of the antichrist, which you have heard is coming and even now is already in the world (1 John 4:2, 3).*

The teaching that matter is evil while the soul is good is contrary to the Word of God. The soul of man apart from Christ, including his heart and mind, is basically evil.

> *[9]The **heart** is deceitful above all things . . . . [10]I the Lord search the heart and examine the mind, to reward a man according to his conduct (Jeremiah 17:9, 10).*

> *[28]. . ., since they did not think it worthwhile to retain the knowledge of God, He gave them over to a depraved **mind** . . . [29]They have become filled with every kind of wickedness, evil, greed and depravity . . . (Romans 1:28, 29).*

♦   What does Jeremiah say the heart is? _____

♦   What adjective does the book of Romans use to describe the mind? _____

The Scriptures teach that both body and soul have been contaminated by sin. Sin originates in the soul (heart, mind) and is carried out in the body.

> *The **soul** who sins is the one who will die (Ezekiel 18:20).*

> *[14]But each one is tempted when, by his own evil desire, he is dragged away and enticed. [15]Then, after **desire** has conceived, it gives birth to sin; and sin, when it is full-grown, gives birth to death (James 1:14-15).*

The very soul of man is sinful. The aim of the gospel is to convert the soul through repentance, faith, and the new birth. God requires repentance (a change of mind and heart) for forgiveness of sins.

Although both body and soul have been contaminated by sin, matter is not inherently evil. If it were, Jesus could not have come in the flesh. If matter were evil, then the goal of our salvation would be to rid ourselves of it. We would then be headed for annihilation of the body rather than resurrection; Nirvana instead of Heaven. But the Scriptures are plain—as surely as the soul is converted, the body will be resurrected.

♦   What evidence from God's Word can you present to prove that matter is not inherently evil?

♦   Why is this important to the discussion on celibacy?

Sex Within Marriage is
Not Degrading to the Body

God said that the world he made was "good." Not all activities of the flesh are evil. There are activities of the soul that are good (praise, worship, thanksgiving, etc.). In the same way, there are activities of the body that are good. Sex *within marriage* is one such activity. There is nothing immoral or degrading about it. The book of Proverbs advises the young man:

> *15Drink water from your own cistern,*
> *running water from your own well ...*
> *18May your fountain be blessed,*
> *and may you rejoice in the **wife** of your youth.*
> *19A loving doe, a graceful deer—*
> *may her breasts satisfy you always,*
> *may you ever be captivated by her love ...*
> *(Proverbs 5:15-19).*

One entire book of the Old Testament (The Song of Songs, eight chapters) is a celebration of sexual love between two **married** lovers.

> *6How beautiful you are and how pleasing,*
> *O love, with your delights!*
> *7Your stature is like that of the palm,*
> *and your breasts like clusters of fruit.*
> *8I said, "I will climb the palm tree;*
> *I will take hold of its fruit*
> *(Song of Songs 7:6-8).*

God does not view sexual love **between husband and wife** to be a *"necessary evil for the propagation of mankind."* Rather he sees it as beautiful, poetic!

Jesus Did Not Command the Twelve Disciples to Remain Single

Some seek to justify the law of celibacy saying that God's priests should imitate the Lord Jesus in all things. Jesus is the supreme example of godly living and those who want to live godly lives should imitate Him. Since Jesus did not marry, clergy should not marry either.

This all sounds very spiritual. However, Jesus is the divine Son of God; we are not. He saves people from their sins; we cannot. We follow Him as disciples, not as saviors; as humans, not as gods. When it comes to marriage, we are **commanded** to follow His **teaching,** but we are **not commanded** to imitate His celibacy. Clergy may choose to remain single if God enables them to do so, but Jesus never taught that they must.

Some people object that priestly and religious celibacy is something unknown at the time of Christ, and is, therefore, a later development in the Church by the will of God. Nothing is more untrue! During Jesus' time the Essenes practiced celibacy in a kind of community life. If a celibate community life were the ideal, Jesus would have advised His followers to practice it. He did not.

Other Catholics may object that Jesus did command His disciples to live as celibates when He said:

> *Anyone who loves his father or mother more than me is not worthy of me; anyone who loves his son or daughter more than me is not worthy of me (Matthew 10:37).*

Obviously this cannot mean that one is not supposed to have parents! It also cannot mean that one should not have wife or children, because one cannot love wife or children more than Jesus, if he hasn't got any! The context of Christ's words is preaching and the acceptance of the Gospel. If parents or wife or children hinder one from believing in Christ and following Him, then one must choose Christ in spite of possible persecutions and divisions (see verses 34-36 and 38-39).

Nowhere in the New Testament does Jesus command any of His followers not to marry. In fact, the majority of those He chose were married men.

Most of the Twelve Disciples Were Married Men

Three of the four Gospel writers tell of a time when Jesus healed Peter's *mother-in-law*. It happened during Jesus' ministry in Galilee, in the town of Capernaum where many striking miracles took place. In Capernaum Jesus healed the centurion's palsied servant (Matthew 8:5-13), the paralytic who was lowered through the roof by three friends (Mark 2:1-13), a nobleman's son (John 4:46-54), and many others who were sick or demon-possessed. Jesus had made Capernaum His headquarters during this year of popularity (Matthew 4:13; Mark 2:1). Simon and his brother Andrew had a house there. Matthew the tax collector was also a resident there. One day Jesus, along with James and John, visited Simon Peter's home and found Peter's mother-in-law sick with fever. He took her by the hand, helped her to her feet, and immediately the fever left her (Matthew 8:14; Mark 1:30; Luke 4:38). It would be difficult for Jesus to heal Simon Peter's mother-in-law if Peter were not married. The apostle Peter himself (allegedly the first Catholic Pope) was a married man!

Peter was not the only one of the early apostles who was married. Paul, in defending his own rights as an apostle, points out that "the other apostles" received support, not just for themselves, but also for their *wives* (1 Corinthians 9:5). They, too, were married men!

Mary, the Mother of Jesus, Did Not Remain Single

In order to support their law of celibacy, the Roman Catholic Church portrays Mary as a perpetual virgin in spite of the fact that the Scripture teaches the contrary. She was a virgin only until the birth of Jesus. After that she lived as a wife to Joseph:[1]

> *²⁴When Joseph woke up, he did what the angel of the Lord commanded him and took Mary home as his wife. ²⁵But he had no union with her **until** she gave birth to a son (Matthew 1:24-25).*

♦ What did Joseph do with Mary after the angel appeared to him?

♦ How do we know that it was God's will for Joseph and Mary to get married and live as husband and wife?

The Roman Catholic Law of Celibacy Is Not Supported by the Apostle's Teaching

Those passages of Scripture praising celibacy, and even encouraging it under certain circumstances, are fully accepted and followed by true believers (see Matthew 19:11,12; 1 Corinthians 7). The Roman Catholic Law of Celibacy, however, is extreme and should be rejected by true believers because it is contrary to the teaching of God's Word:

> *¹Now for the matters you wrote about: It is good for a man not to marry. But since there is so much immorality,*

---

[1]For more information on this subject, see chapter 9, *"The Truth About Mary."*

each man should have his own wife, and each woman her own husband . . . . [7]I wish that all men were as I am [having self-control]. *But each man has his own gift from God; one has this gift, another has that. [8]Now to the unmarried and the widows I say: It is good for them to stay unmarried, as I am. [9]But if they cannot control themselves, they should marry, for it is better to marry than to burn with passion (1 Corinthians 7:1-9).*

[10]The disciples said to him, "If this is the situation between a husband and a wife, it is better not to marry." [11]Jesus replied, "Not everyone can accept this word, but only those to whom it has been given. [12]For some are eunuchs because they were born that way; others were made that way by men; and others have renounced marriage because of the kingdom of heaven. The one who can accept this should accept it" (Matthew 19:10-12).

The Teaching of the Word of God Concerning Celibacy	The Teaching of the Catholic Church Concerning Celibacy
Celibacy is a good option.	Celibacy is the only option.
In most cases, marriage is advised.	In the case of a priest, marriage is never advised. It is forbidden.
Only those who have the gift of celibacy are expected to remain single.	All priests are expected to remain single, whether they have the gift of celibacy or not.
Marriage is better than celibacy for those who burn with passion.	Marriage is forbidden to priests, even to those who burn with passion.
Celibacy can be chosen by some (those who can accept it).	Celibacy is imposed on all who will be priests.

♦ Study the comparison above and mark the following statements. Mark those statements that agree with the teaching of the Bible with a "**B**," and those that agree with the teachings of the Catholic church with a "**C**."

____ All clergy must remain single.

____ Any person may choose to remain single if God so enables, but he/she is also free to marry.

____ It is better to be married than to burn with passion.

____ Priests cannot marry, even though they burn with passion.

____ Marriage is the norm, but not the rule. Most people will be married; some may choose to remain single.

God Does Not Require Church Leaders To Be Single

God's Word lists in detail the requisites for church leaders. Celibacy is not included in the list. In fact, the opposite is true. God says:

> *[1]If anyone sets his heart on being an overseer (bishop), he desires a noble task. [2]Now the overseer must be above reproach, the husband of but one wife . . . (1 Timothy 3:1-2).*

This statement of Scripture definitely allows the church leader to be a married man. The desire to be a servant leader is good and noble, but God gives some requirements. One of these is that the overseer must be a faithful husband.

One could argue from this passage that the bishop not only *can* be married, but that he *should*.

> *[4]He [the candidate for bishop] must manage his own family well and see that his children obey him with proper*

respect. ⁵If anyone does not know how to manage his own family, how can he take care of God's church (1 Timothy 3:4, 5)?

The one who is chosen as bishop (pastor) *should* be an exemplary father and husband because he proves that he is qualified to govern the church by the way he governs his family. Roman Catholic Popes, bishops and priests have no opportunity to show whether they have these characteristics! If only the Catholic Church had been guided by the teaching of God's Word, rather than the philosophies of men! God knows best! Human religions sometimes think God's Word is not adequate, and in the long run men will pay dearly for their presumption!

The Church Leader Is Supposed To Be A Role Model To Married Men

---

A CONSEQUENCE OF DEFYING GOD'S WORD

In very many Catholic homes, the husbands and fathers are not the spiritual and religious leaders of their families. Most consider religion an important matter for women and children and leave it to their wives.

I was born into a very Catholic family. I was a Catholic for 39 years and a priest for 13. I have traveled in many different countries. I have known thousands and thousands of Catholic families.

Some may find what I am about to say unbelievable. But it is true. In all my experience with Catholic families, I remember only one in which the father cared for the spiritual welfare of the family by being the spiritual leader. It was not my family!

I see two main reasons why Catholic men are not the spiritual leaders God wants them to be at home: (1) the sacramental priesthood, which has deprived Catholics of their own priesthood, and (2) the law of celibacy, which has segregated priests from the normal lives of husbands and fathers.

The church leader, with all the characteristics God requires of him, is supposed to be a role model of a Christian husband and father! Men in the church should be able to look up to their pastor as an example to follow in their own relationships with their wives and children and in their responsibility to be the spiritual leader in the family.

The pastor often will be required to give guidance to married couples who are having difficulty adjusting in their relationship with each other or in training their children. Will not the pastor himself be better equipped as their counselor, more able to understand and to empathize, if he is a married man as God permits him to be? Will it not be easier for married couples to seek guidance from a pastor who not only has theoretical knowledge, but also practical experience?

God Has Not Sanctioned The Monastery As An Institution

In the Catholic Church there are two different kinds of priests: the secular or diocesan and the regular or religious. The first live alone or with relatives, make only the vow of celibacy, and are directly accountable to their bishop. They are called secular because they live in the world (*saeculum*).

The second kind of priest is the regular or religious. These belong to one of the many recognized religious orders or congregations of the Catholic Church such as the Franciscans, Dominicans, Jesuits, Salesians, and Augustinians. The religious are called regular because they live under a rule (*regula*). They make three vows of poverty, celibacy and obedience; they live in communities. Laymen and women can be members of religious orders as lay monks or nuns.

The Roman Catholic Church calls religious or monastic life a state of perfection where people lead a holier life because of their vows and rules. It is also declared a canonical or officially instituted state of life, with privileges recognized by law in most countries.

I would dare to say that the very foundation and main premise of religious life and vows is contrary to God's will. In monastic life, young men and women get out of the world in order to avoid temptation and lead a holier life! Jesus says:

> *Go into all the world and preach the good news to all creation (Mark 16:15).*

> *My prayer is not that you take them out of the world but that you protect them from the evil one (John 17:15).*

♦ Read the following verses.

> *13You are the salt of the earth. But if the salt loses its saltiness, how can it be made salty again? It is no longer good for anything, except to be thrown out and trampled by men. 14You are the light of the world. A city on a hill cannot be hidden. 15Neither do people light a lamp and put it under a bowl. Instead they put it on its stand, and it gives light to everyone in the house. 16In the same way, let your light shine before men, that they may see your good deeds and praise your Father in heaven (Matthew 5:13-16).*

♦ According to the verses quoted above, how does God expect His people to relate to the world? Choose two.

    ____ He wants them to hide from it.

    ____ He wants them to preserve it as salt preserves meat.

    ____ He wants them to be light in the darkness.

    ____ He does not want them to have anything to do with the world.

In the Bible we know of only three official institutions ordained by God: the family (Matthew 19:4-6; Colossians 3:18-21), the church (Matthew 16:18; Hebrews 13:7,17), and the state (Romans 14:1,2; 1 Peter 2:13-14). Within these institutions believers are to exercise their gifts and grow in holiness, love of God and love of neighbor.

The Catholic Church has created a fourth institution, the convent or monastery, which it describes as a "more thorough-going way" of life. They refer to these convents as "religious families." These priests, monks, and nuns are supposed to attain Christian perfection by keeping vows and obeying rules and superiors. In the Vatican II documents the Catholic Church declares:

> *Besides giving legal sanction to the religious [monastic] form of life and thus raising it to the dignity of a canonical state . . . the church, in virtue of her God-given authority, receives the vows of those who profess this form of life (No. 28, Lumen Gentium).*

Where and when was the authority given to set up a "better" form of life than the family which God established? God did **not** say "For this reason a man will leave his father and mother and join a monastery!" He said: *For this reason a man will leave his father and mother and be united with his wife (Matthew 19:4)!*

Can the Church do better than God by exhorting bachelors to live together like a family? This is simply presumptuous! It is surely the root of many moral disorders and sexual anomalies (sins!) in so many monasteries of priests, monks and nuns, and so many seminaries! For centuries these immoral events were kept secret, but lately numerous victims have begun to reveal the truth. Certainly God would rather his servant leaders be married than fall into sin. Thus, he says through the apostle Paul:

> [8]*To the unmarried and the widows I say: It is good for them to stay unmarried, as I am.* [9]*But **if they cannot control themselves, they should marry,** for it is better to marry than to burn with passion (1 Corinthians 7:8-9).*

The celibacy Paul advocates is a gift and an option, but it is an option only if it will not result in sin! A life of celibacy, if it is God's gift, should be lived in the regular form of life God has established.

A Christian Woman Does Not Need To Be A Virgin To Become The Bride Of Christ

Here is another misleading and false statement of Roman Catholicism:

> *Similar to these forms of consecrated life is the order of virgins who, hearkening the sacred call to follow Christ more closely, are consecrated to God by the diocesan bishop and are mystically espoused to Christ! (The Consecrated Life, 9th Synod of Bishops, 1993)*

The words "more closely" point to a comparison between matrimony (a God-ordained state of life) and the monastery (a man-made institution). The 9th Synod of Bishops dares to describe the Catholic way as "better" than God's way.

The statement that the virgins are "mystically espoused to Christ" is an outright lie. God's Word teaches that God rejoices over *all* his people as a bridegroom rejoices over the bride:

> *For your Maker is your husband—the LORD Almighty is His name (Isaiah 54:5).*

> *As a bridegroom rejoices over his bride, so will God rejoice over you (Isaiah 62:5b).*

The Bride of Christ is the Church. All believers! Not just nuns!

> *Let us rejoice and be glad and give him glory! For the wedding of the Lamb has come, and his bride [The church] has made herself ready (Revelation 19:7).*

♦ Who is the bride of Christ according to the Scriptures?

Celibacy Is Not The Sacrifice Of Happiness
For The Sake Of Holiness

Catholicism presents celibacy as a form of self-denial and sacrifice in imitation of Christ. Priests, monks, and nuns, through celibacy, embrace a life of loneliness and suffering, giving up the joys of marriage and family. This is the sacrifice of their lives for their salvation and sanctification, and for the salvation of souls.

Rev. Richard Bennett, a former Dominican priest who is now a true believer, in his article *"Is the Monastic Man-Made?"* writes:

> *My first years as a monk, eighteen years old, I remember Archbishop Finbar Ryan coming to the novitiate. In intensely dramatic tones, for which he was known, he spoke of the cup of suffering that must be filled. "Mary's heart was pierced unto blood, then Joseph's, Jude's and the Apostles', Dominic's, Francis', Aquinas', and Catherine's. They have put their drops of blood into this cup. Now it is your turn." In his hand was an imaginary cup which he passed in front of the awe-struck novice monks! Later in a separate talk, he spoke of the zeal of the Hitler youth towards the end of the war. He spoke of a Churchillian cry for more than blood, sweat and tears, a call to lay down our lives in sacrifice as did Christ Jesus for the salvation of souls.*

The belief that we can save people from hell through the sacrifice of our lives, by renouncing marriage, appeals to our spiritual pride and offers incentive for suffering what the Catholic law of celibacy demands. It is, however, a most unbiblical teaching. As we have seen in previous chapters, Jesus has offered the only sacrifice for sin! There is no need for us to renounce marriage in order to save souls from hell.

♦ How did Archbishop Finbar Ryan seek to motivate those at the novitiate to renounce marriage?

Conclusion

♦ When did the Roman Catholic Church impose celibacy on all priests (see p. 115)?

♦ What was the main reason for this decision (see p. 116)?

♦ How did Gnosticism lead to the conviction that "sexual activity was *a necessary evil* for the propagation of mankind" (see p. 116)?

♦ What led certain false teachers in the apostle John's time to conclude that Jesus Christ did not come in the flesh (see p. 116)?

♦ How does the teaching of the apostle John contradict the idea that matter is evil (see 1 John 4:2-3, p. 116)?

♦ Where does sin originate: in the soul or in the body (see p. 117)?

♦ How are we tempted according to James 1:14-15 (see p. 117)?

♦ What kind of love do the passages Proverbs 5:15-19 and Song of Songs 7:6-7 speak of (see p. 118)?

♦ What does God mean when he commands: *Drink from your own cistern ... may you rejoice in the wife of your youth* (Proverbs 5:15-19)?

♦ Why do you think Jesus did not marry?
      _____ His mother would not let him.
      _____ Because marriage is a necessary evil and would have defiled him.
      _____ Because He was the Son of God.
      _____ Other:

♦ Just before God created Eve, He said: *It is not good for the man* [Adam] *to be alone. I will make a helper suitable for him (Genesis 2:18).* Write "A" for *agree* and "D" for *disagree* beside each of the following statements:
      _____ God instituted marriage because He knew it was not good for a man to be alone.
      _____ It is not a good thing for a man of God to have a wife.
      _____ God intends marriage to satisfy our needs for intimacy and companionship.
      _____ It is good for a man **not** to be alone.

♦ What evidence is there in the Scriptures to prove that Peter was a married man (see p. 120)?

♦ What verse of Scripture indicates that the other apostles were also married men (see p. 120)?

♦ What is the second qualification in the list of qualifications in 1 Timothy 3 for being a bishop or overseer (see p. 123)?

♦ Why should a bishop (overseer) be a family man according to 1 Timothy 3:4, 5 (see pp. 123-124)?

♦ How does 1 Timothy 3:4, 5 contradict the Catholic law of celibacy?

♦ If you were trying to explain the wisdom of God on this issue to a bishop or priest, what would you say to him?

♦ The two kinds of priests in the Catholic Church are the
_____ and the _____ (see p. 125).

♦ The Catholic Church views religious or monastic life as a state of _____ where people lead a _____ life according to their vows and rules (see p. 125).

♦ Read Matthew 5:13-16 then draw a line between the activity on the left and the corresponding metaphor on the right.

Being examples in an ungodly world	Hiding your light under a bowl
Isolating ourselves from the world	Being salt that has lost its saltiness
Promoting righteousness and justice	Letting your light shine
Living like the world lives	Living as salt of the earth

♦ What is the best way for you to live as salt and light?
   ____ To isolate myself from the world and live in a convent
   ____ To live in the world without living like the world

♦ What are the three institutions God has established (see p. 126)?

♦ How is the celibacy Paul advocates different from monastic life (see p. 128)?

♦ God would rather his servant leaders be married than fall into _____ (see p. 127)!

♦ Write a prayer in the space below thanking God for his gifts to you (a wife, a husband, the gift of celibacy). Thank Him for understanding your needs, and providing for them.

Chapter 10

The Truth About Mary

I n the fall of 1982, while teaching at Western Seminary in Portland, Oregon, I befriended a former Roman Catholic priest named Ted. He had been wounded while serving as a chaplain in the Vietnam war, and had to return to America. He left the priesthood in frustration. He was open to dialogue with Evangelicals, but said he would never join them for one single reason: Evangelicals did not believe in Mary and pray to her.

I showed him several Bible passages to prove that we Evangelicals were right. He said he had already heard all that stuff. And he continued: *"If Jesus Christ, who is the son of Mary in His human nature, is so powerful, why do you think His mother is good for nothing?"*

I assured him that far from thinking that Mary is "good for nothing," we count her blessed among all women. She, alone, was privileged to be the mother of our Redeemer. Seeing that his attachments were more emotional than doctrinal, I decided to use the following example to help him understand:

"Suppose you are found to have stomach cancer, and the doctors urgently suggest surgery. They take you to the hospital and prepare you, but before the anesthesiologist puts you under, the nurse approaches and whispers:

'Sir, the surgeon is not here, but his mother is around!'
'Is his mother a surgeon, too?'
'No, she is a lawyer. But if her son is such a good surgeon, do you expect his mother to be good for nothing?' "

This illustrates the folly of attributing to Mary what belongs only to her Son, Jesus. And yet, it has happened.

The Roman Catholic Church the world over has given a place of preeminence to Mary both in doctrine and practice. In this chapter we will answer some of the most commonly asked questions concerning Mary and the Church's teaching about her.

What Was Mary's Role As The Mother Of Jesus?

Anyone who reads the New Testament carefully will see Mary's unique role in the coming of Messiah into this world. Scripture is absolutely clear in stating that Mary was the true mother of Jesus Christ according to His human nature. The account in the Gospel of Luke leaves no room for any doubt about this fact:

26In the sixth month of Elizabeth's pregnancy, God sent the angel Gabriel to a town in Galilee named Nazareth. 27He had a message for a girl promised in marriage to a man named Joseph, who was a descendant of King David. The girl's name was Mary. 28The angel came to her and said, "Peace be with you! The Lord is with you and has greatly blessed you!"

[29]Mary was deeply troubled by the angel's message, and she wondered what his words meant. [30]The angel said to her, "Don't be afraid, Mary; God has been gracious to you. [31]You will become pregnant and give birth to a son, and you will name him Jesus. [32]He will be great and will be called the Son of the Most High God. The Lord God will make him a king, as his ancestor David was, [33]and he will be the king of the descendants of Jacob forever; His kingdom will never end!"

[34]Mary said to the angel, "I am a virgin. How, then, can this be?"

[35]The angel answered, "The Holy Spirit will come on you, and God's power will rest upon you. For this reason the holy child will be called the Son of God" (Luke 1:26-35, TEV).

Luke also records the following encounter between Mary and her cousin Elizabeth:

[41]When Elizabeth heard Mary's greeting, the baby leaped in her womb, and Elizabeth was filled with the Holy Spirit. [42]In a loud voice she exclaimed: "Blessed are you among women, and blessed is the child you will bear! [43]But why am I so favored, that the mother of my Lord should come to me?" (Luke 1:41-43).

Elizabeth, filled with the Holy Spirit, called Mary "the mother of my Lord." From the moment of His conception in the womb of Mary, Jesus was Lord and God.

The writers of the Old and New Testaments were privileged to be used of the Holy Spirit to deliver God's written and infallible Word, the Bible. Mary was privileged even more. God used her, not just to deliver a written word, but the living and incarnate Word, Jesus.

As the mother of Jesus, Mary witnessed many of the important events in Christ's life. She also suffered much for His sake, from the time of His conception until His crucifixion. When she and Joseph presented Jesus in the temple, Simeon blessed them and said to Mary:

> *34. . . "This child is chosen by God for the destruction and salvation of many in Israel. He will be a sign from God which many people will speak against 35and so reveal their secret thoughts. And sorrow, like a sharp sword, will break your own heart" (Luke 2:34-35, TEV).*

Simeon addressed Mary, not her husband Joseph as was customary among the Jews. The old man, filled with the Holy Spirit, knew that Jesus was not Joseph's son, but Mary's. Mary was truly the mother of Jesus in His humanity.

Is Mary the "Mother of God"?

Jesus is more than just a man. He is truly God, the second person of the Trinity, the eternal Son through whom all things were created. As God, He had no beginning, and He was Mary's Creator. As God, He cannot possibly have a mother. Mary cannot be the mother of God the Father, nor the mother of God the Holy Spirit. In the same way, she is **not** the mother of God the Son.

Yet millions of people call Mary "the mother of God" and pray to her as such. They justify this by saying that she is the true mother of Jesus, and since Jesus is God, she is the

The phrase "mother of God" was adopted by the Council of Ephesus to define the Biblical doctrine of incarnation. The title was a very sad and wrong choice of words, as the ensuing centuries would show.

mother of God. They simply fail to distinguish between the human and divine natures of Jesus.

The expression "mother of God" is not found in Scripture. Mary is called the mother of Jesus (Matthew 1:18; 2:11, 13, 14, 20, 21; 12:46, 47; Mark 3:31, 32; Luke 2:34; 8:19, 20; John 2:1, 3, 12; 6:42; 19:26). Once Elizabeth referred to her as "the mother of my Lord." But never is she called the "mother of God."

The term "mother of God" was used for the first time in the fifth century, during the Council of Ephesus (AD 431). The Council fathers, and later the Greek Orthodox, called Mary the "God-bearer";[1] the Romans preferred to call her "mother of God."[2]

The Council of Ephesus sought to define the Biblical doctrine of the incarnation. They were responding to some who taught wrongly that Jesus was not God from the moment of His conception. The Council settled on the phrase "mother of God" to show that Jesus did not become God, but that Jesus, as God, became man. The Council rightly affirmed that in the incarnation God became man, not vice versa. The phrase "mother of God" was adopted to uphold the idea that Jesus was truly God from the moment He was conceived by the Holy Spirit. This was definitely a very sad and wrong choice of words, as the ensuing centuries would show.

Because of this title, people began to look at Mary as someone more than human. They began to say that Mary could not possibly have been a sinner at any moment of her life, and that her body could not have possibly undergone corruption because that would not be fitting for the mother of God. And, of course, many began to pray to her.

The phrase "Mother of God" states that Mary is the mother of Jesus-as-God. Both Evangelicals and the official doctrine of the Catholic Church teach that this is not true.

---

[1] θεοτοκος in the Greek.
[2] Dei Genitrix or Mater Dei.

Is It Right To Pray To Mary?

Mary is a human being and a believer. Like all other departed believers, her spirit is now with the Lord. Mary is not a goddess, and there is nothing to justify praying to her. In Scripture, there is absolutely no example of anyone praying to a dead saint. There is good reason for this: the human being who dies and goes to be with the Lord is still human. Mary is not omniscient, omnipresent, nor omnipotent. She cannot hear and answer prayer.

There are about 900 million people in the world who believe, according to their Church's teaching, that Mary is the mother of God and that, therefore, they can pray to her. It is quite possible that there may be two, three, or even ten million people scattered all over the world praying to Mary at the same time, in many different languages, and asking for a great variety of things. In order for Mary to hear and answer all those prayers, she should be omnipresent, omniscient, and omnipotent.

Prayer is one of the deepest forms of worship, because prayer acknowledges the full power of the person to whom we pray. People who pray to Mary, though they call such activity venerating or honoring, are in fact worshiping her.

> **Prayer is one of the deepest forms of worship, because prayer acknowledges the full power of the person to whom we pray.**

Consider one of the most popular Roman Catholic prayers in honor of Mary, "Hail Holy Queen," attributed to Alphonsus Liguori, a famous Roman Catholic bishop who has been canonized as a saint.

The prayer begins:

"Hail, Holy Queen ..."

However, the Bible says:

God alone is holy.
Jesus alone reigns.
(Revelation 15:4; 17:14; 19:18)

Nowhere in the Scriptures is Mary called "holy," and nowhere is she called "Queen." Roman Catholics often refer to Mary as the "Queen of Heaven."

Roman Catholics often refer to Mary as the "Queen of Heaven." The only one called by that name in the Bible is Ishtar or Ashtoreth, the wife of the Babylonian idol god Baal.

The only one called by that name in the Bible is Ishtar or Ashtoreth, the wife of the Babylonian idol god Baal (Jeremiah 44:17-19).

The prayer to Mary continues:

"Hail, our life, our sweetness, our hope . . ."

The Bible says:

> *Jesus alone is our life.*
> *Jesus alone is our hope*
> (John 11:25; 14:6; Colossians 1:27).

This same prayer also addresses Mary as our advocate:

"Turn then, most gracious Advocate . . ."

The Bible says:

> *Jesus alone is our advocate.*
> (1 John 2:2; 1 Timothy 2:5).

Study Jesus' teaching about prayer in the following passages. To whom did Jesus teach us to pray?

> *This, then, is how you should pray: Our Father in heaven . . . (Matthew 6:9).*

> *He said to them, "When you pray, say: 'Father . . .' "*
> *(Luke 11:2).*

> *If you, then, though you are evil, know how to give
> good gifts to your children, how much more will your
> Father in heaven give good gifts to those who ask him!*
> (Matthew 7:11).

Study the prayers of Jesus in the verses below. To whom
did Jesus pray?

> *After Jesus said this, he looked toward heaven and prayed:
> "Father . . ." (Luke 17:1).*

> *At that time Jesus said, "I praise you Father . . ."*
> (Matthew 11:25).

♦ 1 Timothy 2:5 says that "there is _____ mediator
between God and man." He is _____ _____.
1 John 2:2 says that Jesus Christ is our advocate with the
Father.

♦ John 11:25 says that Jesus is the _____ and the
_____.

♦ Colossians 1:27 says that "Christ in you" is "the _____
of glory."

♦ Revelation 15:4 says that God alone is _____.

According to the verses listed above from God's Word, state
what is wrong with the following well-known and officially
approved prayer to Mary.

> *Hail, Holy Queen,*
> *Mother of Mercy*
> *Hail, our life, our sweetness, our hope.*
> *Turn, then, most gracious advocate . . . .*

Was Mary A Perpetual Virgin?

At the end of the fourth century, the Roman Catholic Church had already begun to teach Mary's perpetual virginity.[3] The dogma says that Mary remained a virgin all her life, did not become Joseph's wife, and never had any children by him. Her only offspring was Jesus, who was conceived miraculously by the Holy Spirit.

This dogma exalts the purity of Mary, her faithfulness to God, and the truth of the Virgin Birth. These we accept. But, the Scriptures clearly teach that Mary had other children besides Jesus. The names of four brothers of Jesus are recorded in Mark 6:3:

> *"Isn't he the carpenter, the son of Mary, and the brother of James, Joseph, Judas, and Simon? Aren't his sisters living here?" And so they rejected him (TEV).*

These were definitely half-brothers and half-sisters, since Joseph was not Jesus' father. Some people say that the phrase "brothers and sisters" could mean cousins or relatives. We know this cannot be true from the context of the passage and the words used. There are words for "cousin" and "relative" in Greek, but the words used mean "brothers and sisters."

In addition, there are other important passages where the brothers of Jesus are mentioned. We find the following in the

---

[3] *Letter of Pope Siricius to Anysius, Bishop of Thessalonica, AD 392,* cited by Neuner, Roos, and Rahner, S.J., *The Teaching of the Catholic Church* (Stanton Island: Alba Press, 1967), p. 183. "Your Holiness is rightly repelled by the idea that any other birth should have taken place from the womb whence Christ was born according to the flesh. Jesus would not have chosen to be born of a virgin if He had had to regard her as being so little continent as to desecrate the place of birth of the Lord's body, that temple of the eternal King, by human intercourse . . ." Notice that the logical basis for this doctrine is the assumption that sex within marriage desecrates! The doctrine of perpetual virginity was made official at the Council of Trent (1547).

Gospel of Matthew. It is also recorded by Mark:

> *⁴⁶Jesus was still talking to the people when his mother and brothers arrived. They stood outside, asking to speak with Him. ⁴⁷So one of the people there said to him, "Look, your mother and brothers are standing outside, and they want to speak with you." ⁴⁸Jesus answered, "Who is my mother? Who are my brothers?" ⁴⁹Then He pointed to His disciples and said, "Look! Here are my mother and my brothers! ⁵⁰Whoever does what my Father in heaven wants him to do is my brother, my sister, and my mother"* (Matthew 12:46-50 TEV).

A careful look at the intentions of Jesus in this passage will prove beyond all doubt that these were real brothers and sisters, not just distant relatives or disciples. Jesus is teaching about the intimate spiritual relationship that exists between Himself and His followers. He is saying that the spiritual relationship He has with His disciples is much deeper and more lasting than the physical relationship He has with His mother and His brothers. If these were not brothers, but merely distant relatives or disciples, then the strength of the argument is gone.

Some quote Matthew 1:24, 25 to try to prove that Mary had no children after Jesus:

> *²⁴When Joseph woke up, he did what the angel of the Lord had commanded him and took Mary home as his wife. ²⁵But he had no union with her until she gave birth to a son. And he gave him the name Jesus (NIV).*

This passage says that Joseph kept Mary a virgin *until* Jesus was born, but it does not suggest that he kept her a virgin *after* that. In fact, the word "until" implies the opposite. Joseph *"took Mary home as his wife."* In the Jewish culture, (and in any culture for that matter), it is inconceivable that a man would marry a girl without exercising his conjugal right.

♦ How many brothers (half-brothers, born to Mary and Joseph) did Jesus have according to Mark 6:3? What are their names?

♦ How do we know that Jesus had more than one half-sister?

♦ Who was waiting outside to see Jesus in the episode of Matthew 12:46-48?

♦ How does Matthew 1:24, 25 give support to the idea that Jesus may have had half-brothers?

Was Mary Immaculately Conceived?

Another dogma of the Catholic Church, one that glorifies Mary the most, is the dogma of the Immaculate Conception defined by Pope Pius IX on December 8, 1854.[4] This dogma teaches that Mary was conceived without sin (that is, she

---

[4] Pope Pius IX's Bull *Inefabilis Deus* Proclaiming the Immaculate Conception (8 December 1854). Quoted by Neuner, Roos and Rahner, S.J., *The Teachings of the Catholic Church*, (Stanton Island: Alba Press, 1967), p. 186. "To the glory of the holy and undivided Trinity, to the honour and ornament of the Virgin Mother of God, the exaltation of the Catholic faith and the increase of Christian religion, We, by the authority of our Lord Jesus Christ, of the blessed Apostles Peter and Paul, and by Our own authority declare, pronounce and define that the doctrine which holds that the Most Blessed Virgin Mary from the first moment of her conception was, by the singular grace and privilege of Almighty God, in view of the merits of Christ Jesus the Savior of the human race, preserved immune from all stain of original sin, is revealed by God and is, therefore, firmly and constantly to be believed by all the faithful. Wherefore, if any persons shall dare to think, which God forbid, otherwise than has been defined by Us, let them clearly

had no original sin), and that she never sinned throughout her life.

The Bible says: *All have sinned and fall short of God's glory* (Romans 3:23). The only exception the Bible makes is Jesus Christ (Hebrews 4:15).

Mary was highly favored by God, but she was not without sin.

If Mary never sinned, she did not need a Savior. However, Mary, herself, in her beautiful song of praise in Luke chapter one, rejoiced that she had a Savior:

> [46]*My soul exalts the Lord,* [47]*and my spirit has rejoiced in God, my Savior (Luke 1:46, 47).*

The Catholic Church tries to prove that Mary was conceived without sin by saying that only someone who was sinless could have given birth to a sinless one. It is easy to see the fallacy of this logic because then Mary must have had sinless parents, grandparents and ancestors to have been conceived without sin.

Writing about the dogma of the immaculate conception, Joseph Zacchello, a former Catholic priest, points out in his book, *Secret of Romanism*:

> Even Tradition, the usual refuge of Roman Catholics, contradicts this papal dogma. Augustine, Ambrose, Chrysostom, Eusebius, Anselm, Cardinal Cajetan, St. Antoninus, St. Thomas Aquinas, Pope Gregory the Great, Pope Innocent III, and many other Fathers, doctors, saints, and the Popes of the Roman Church clearly deny that Mary was conceived without original sin.[5]

know that they are condemned by their own judgment, that they have suffered shipwreck to their faith and fallen from the unity of the Church, that they thenceforth subject themselves *ipso facto* to the penalties provided by law if they shall dare to express their views in speech or writing or in any other way."

[5] Joseph Zacchello, *Secret of Romanism*.

Mary was highly favored, and extended great mercy, when she was chosen to be the mother of Jesus.[6] But she was not without original sin.

The Roman Catholic Church contends that Mary needed to be sinless in order for Jesus to be conceived without sin. If that is true, and Mary is sinless, then are her parents sinless also? And what about her parents' parents? The doctrine of the Immaculate Conception of Mary does not solve the problem of how a sinful person could give birth to a sinless one. It only pushes the problem back one generation, and actually makes the problem worse. Jesus is the unique Son of God, born of a virgin and conceived by the Holy Spirit. He is sinless because He is divine. Mary is not divine, and she was not born of a virgin, nor conceived by the Holy Spirit.

Is Mary the Mediatrix of All Grace?

According to the Roman Catholic Church, as taught in the encyclicals of Pope Leo XIII [7] and Pope Pius X, [8] Mary is the

---

[6] Some theologians offer Luke 1:38 as proof of the immaculate conception. The phrase "full of grace" (Κεχαριτωμενη) means "highly favored." God showed her so much favor (literally grace, Χαρις) that she is described as being filled with it. This does not imply or in any way prove that she was sinless.

[7] Pope Leo XIII's Encyclical *Octobri Mense* (1891), quoted by Neuner, Roos, and Rahner, S.J., *The Teaching of the Catholic Church,* (Stanton Island: Alba Press, 1967), page 187. "Whence ... from that great treasure of grace which the Lord brought ... nothing comes to us except, by God's will, through Mary; so that, just as no one can attain to the supreme Father except through the Son, to a certain extent, no one can attain to the Son except through the Mother .... If, therefore, the awareness of our actions cause us to tremble, we need an advocate and a protector, who is powerful before God in his grace, but who is also so full of goodness that no one, even in the greatest despair, will be refused his protection, and that he will inspire new confidence in God's mercy in all who are oppressed and bowed to earth. Mary is such a one, Mary worthy of all praise; she is the powerful mother, mother of the all-powerful God ... He (Christ) freely willed to be subject to her and to obey her as a child obeys its mother ...We should place ourselves under her protection and loyalty, together with our plans

"Mediatrix of All Grace." This teaching is contrary to the explicit teaching of Scripture. We read in 1 Timothy 2:5:

> *There is one God and **one mediator** between God and men, the man Christ Jesus (NIV).*

Now some Catholic charismatics say, "Mary is not really a mediatrix between us and God. She is only a mediatrix between us and Jesus Christ. She leads us to Christ, whereas Christ leads us to God." And many Catholics use the slogan: "To Jesus, through Mary."

This is not the official teaching of the Roman Catholic Church. The official teaching is that Mary is, like Jesus, a mediatrix between God and sinners. But even if she were a mediatrix between Jesus and sinners, sinners *would*, nevertheless, go through her on the way to God. And since it is claimed that she is the mediatrix of *all* grace, sinners *must* go through her on their way to God.

God

↑

Jesus, the only mediator

↑

Sinners

Wherever you insert Mary in the diagram above, whether between Jesus and sinners, or alongside of Jesus, she becomes a mediator between God and man. God's Word says there cannot be two mediators; there is only one (1 Timothy 2:5).

---

and deeds, our purity and our penance, our sorrows and joys and pleas and wishes. All that is ours we should entrust to her . . . ."

[8] Pope Pius X's *Encyclical Ad Diem Illum* to mark the fiftieth anniversary of the proclamation of the immaculate conception (1904), quoted by Neuner, Roos, and Rahner, S.J., *The Teaching of the Catholic Church*, (Stanton Island: Alba Press, 1967), p. 190. "So intimately had she (Mary) participated in his passion that, had it been possible, she would rather have taken upon herself all the sufferings her Son bore (Bonaventure). This community of suffering and will between Mary and Christ, promoted her to the high dignity of *restorer of the lost world* and thus the dispenser of all the goods which Jesus won for us by his death and at the price of his blood."

Jesus is the *only* one qualified to be our mediator, because He alone is true God and true man. As man, He understands and sympathizes with our weaknesses; as God the Son, He ably represents us to the Father.

Is It True That Mary Was Taken Into Heaven, Body And Soul?

The most recent dogma concerning Mary is referred to as the "assumption of Mary." It was defined in 1950 by Pope Pius XII.[9] It teaches that Mary's body was taken up to heaven together with her soul and spirit.

If the other dogmas were true and biblical, this would be a logical conclusion. Corruption is a consequence of sin. If Mary had no sin, her body would not suffer decay. However, as we have shown, these other dogmas are not true according to the Scriptures.

Is Mary too highly esteemed?

We do count Mary blessed, as the Bible says we should. We praise and thank God for her, and follow her good example as obedient believers. But to go beyond this and attribute powers

---

[9] Pope Pius XII's apostolic constitution *Munificentissimus* (1950), quoted by Neuner, Roos, and Rahner, S.J., *The Teaching of the Catholic Church*, (Stanton Island: Alba Press, 1967), pp. 195-196. "Wherefore, having directed humble and repeated prayers to God, and having invoked the light of the Spirit of Truth, to the glory of Almighty God, who has bestowed his special bounty on the Virgin Mary, for the honour of his Son the immortal King of ages and Victor over sin and death, for the greater glory of his august Mother, and for the joy and exaltation of the whole Church, by the authority of our Lord Jesus Christ, of the blessed Apostles Peter and Paul, and by Our own, We proclaim and define it to be a dogma revealed by God that the immaculate Mother of God, Mary ever Virgin, when the course of her earthly life was finished, was taken up body and soul into the glory of heaven. Wherefore, if anyone, which God forbid, should willfully dare to deny or call in doubt what We have defined, let him know that he has certainly abandoned divine and Catholic faith.

that belong only to God and His Incarnate Son is wrong and even blasphemous. Consider the following chart carefully. Does the Catholic Church attribute to Mary what belongs only to Jesus?

Titles that seem to put Mary on the same level with her Son, Jesus

Jesus	Mary
King of kings	Queen of heaven
One in whom there was no sin	One immaculately conceived
Mediator	Mediatrix of all grace
Redeemer	Co-redemptrix
The hope of glory	Our hope
The life	Our life
Our Advocate	Our Advocate

One of the terrible sins of people is their worship of the creature more than the Creator (Romans 1:25). Many former Roman Catholics testify that they had greater love and devotion for Mary than the Lord Jesus Christ Himself.

Should Followers Of Christ Pray The Rosary?

The most popular practice in honor of Mary is the Rosary. When we consider the Rosary as a prayer, we can see some positive things in it. First of all, the complete Rosary contains the *Lord's Prayer* which is the most beautiful pattern for prayer given by Christ Himself. The Rosary also contains the prayer *Glory be to the Father, to the Son and to the Holy Spirit* . . .

Another very good aspect of the Rosary is the meditation of 15 mysteries or events in the life of Christ or Mary. Thirteen out of 15 of these events are to be found in the Bible; therefore, it is a very good thing that we meditate on these important events in the life of Christ.

On the other hand, the Rosary is a prayer addressed to Mary, in her honor. The "Hail Mary" is recited 150 times throughout. As we have already stated, prayer should be addressed *only* to God.

Parts of the "Hail Mary" can be found in Scripture. It begins with a statement which Gabriel used in greeting Mary.

> Hail [Mary], *full of grace; the Lord is with you.*
> (Luke 1:28)

And then you have Elizabeth's greeting:

> Blessed are you among women and blessed
> is the fruit of your womb.
> (Luke 1:42)

These are found in the Bible, but they are greetings, not prayers.

The second part of the "Hail Mary" is not from the Bible. It has been composed by the Church and contains the unbiblical expressions: "Holy Mary" and "Mother of God."

The Rosary is unacceptable as a prayer because it is addressed to Mary who is a human being like you and me. It is also unacceptable as a prayer because of the constant repetition of words. Jesus had this to say about repetitive prayers:

> When you pray, do not use a lot of meaningless words,
> as the pagans do, who think that their gods will hear
> them because their prayers are long (Matthew 6:7, TEV).

Should Followers Of Jesus Wear A Scapular?

A very common practice among Roman Catholics is the use of scapulars or medals. These are supposed to give the wearer special protection from Mary. Those who have such items with them are entitled to her extraordinary help, grace or assistance at the hour of death.

These scapulars and medals are *substitutes* for the true assurance that we have in Christ. All persons who truly trust in Christ as Savior and Lord of their lives have assurance that they belong to Him. It is Christ's death, resurrection, and His payment for sin that give us assurance that we will be with Him forever. God promises in His Word that He will keep His own and that none who trust in Christ will perish (John 3:18, 36).

It is faith in the heart, not a scapular around the neck, that gives us assurance that we are not condemned. Salvation belongs to those who believe in Jesus, not those who wear a lady's medal.

♦ In Catholic teaching, what promise did Mary allegedly make to all who wear the scapular?

Is It Wrong To Have An Image Of Mary?

If there were an authentic picture or painting of Mary, we could keep it as a remembrance. But there is none. The fact that there exist literally hundreds of different Marys (white, black, and brown, all with different features), shows that there is no true picture of her.

But more serious is the fact that the making of images and using them for prayer, worship, or veneration, is clearly against the commandment of God. For we read in Exodus 20:4,5:

> [4]*Do not make for yourselves images of anything in heaven or on earth or in the water or under the earth.* [5]*Do not bow down to any idol or worship it, because I am the* LORD *your God and I tolerate no rivals (TEV).*

We Love Mary . . . The Biblical Way

We have to thank God for Mary and rejoice because of her. We consider her blessed. Mary is definitely a shining example of how we, as believers, should live. She exemplifies genuine faith, dedication, purity, humility, perseverance, self-denial, and suffering for the sake of Christ. She was knowledgeable of the Scriptures and obedient to its precepts.

However, we must not extol Mary beyond her role as a believer. Most of the dogmas and practices of Catholicism concerning Mary are against the Word of God. Mary, herself, surely would not want us to accept them. She would want us to follow God's Word and to focus on Christ and trust Him alone as our mediator.

♦ What do you think Mary would say to the leaders of the Catholic Church if she were to appear from heaven today?

_____ I am your advocate and the mediatrix of all grace, continue to pray to me and build a shrine in my honor.

_____ I am but a servant of God, like you. Jesus is your advocate. Jesus is your mediator. Take off your scapulars! Tear down the shrines where so many kneel before my image! Stop saying the "Hail Mary." Instead, hail King Jesus. To Him belongs all glory and honor and dominion, now and forevermore!

Conclusion

◆ Mary is an example to believers in many ways. Choose one characteristic of Mary from the list below; tell how she exemplified it and how you intend to imitate her.

____ Humility

____ Obedience

____ Suffering and sacrifice

____ Faith

____ Knowledge of Scripture

____ Prayer

____ Truthfulness

____ Purity

____ Loyalty

____ Faithfulness

____ Courage

◆ Which phrase most accurately describes Mary's relationship to God (see pp. 137-138)?

____ "Mother of God"

____ "Mother of Jesus"

____ "God-bearer"

◆ Which of the following statements is not true of the Son of God (see p. 137)?

____ He created Mary.

____ He was conceived by the Holy Spirit.

____ He has been and is eternally subject to the authority of His human mother, Mary.

____ He became man, born of the virgin Mary.

◆ What attributes or characteristics would Mary need in order to be able to see, hear, understand, and answer the prayers of 10 million people praying to her at the same time in 200 different languages from different locations all around the world (see p. 139)?

____ She would need to be present everywhere in order to see and hear every prayer.

____ She would need to be all-knowing in order to understand every prayer, and to know how best to answer it.

____ She would need supernatural power to be able to answer every prayer.

____ She would not need any supernatural power. Any human being can do these things.

♦ When people pray to Mary, what do they think about her?

____ They assume she can hear and understand them.

____ They assume she can see them.

____ They assume she has the power to answer them.

____ They don't think about whether she has the power to answer.

Turn back to pages 148 and 151, read the truth from God's word. Then read again the Roman Catholic officially approved prayer to Mary. Is there any conflict between this prayer and what God's word says according to 1 Timothy 2:5 and 1 John 2:2?

♦ How does Mary describe her God in Luke 1:47 (see p. 145)?

♦ How does Romans 3:23 contradict the doctrine of the Immaculate Conception of Mary?

♦ What is unique about Jesus, that He alone was conceived without sin?

♦ According to 1 Timothy 2:5, how many mediators are there between God and man (see p. 147)?

♦ Who is the only mediator between God and man (see p. 147)?

    _____ Mary

    _____ Jesus

♦ What powers does the Catholic Church attribute to Mary that belong only to Jesus (see p. 149)?

    _____ None.

    _____ The power to act as mediator between God and man.

    _____ The power to serve as our advocate with the Father.

    _____ The power to redeem.

    _____ The power of a sinless life.

    _____ Other: _____.

♦ How might the attribution of such powers cause people to have greater love for Mary than for Jesus Himself?

♦ How many times is the "Hail Mary" repeated throughout the recitation of the Rosary (see p. 150)?

♦ What unbiblical titles are given to Mary in the Rosary (see p. 150)?

    Mother of _____

    _____ Mary

♦ What did Jesus say about using constant repetition of words in prayer (see p. 150)?

♦ Why is the Rosary unacceptable as a prayer (see p. 150)?

♦ Why do people wear the scapular (see pp. 150-151)?

♦ To whom does God promise eternal life and freedom from eternal punishment (see p. 151)?
    ____ Those who wear the scapular
    ____ Those who believe in Jesus

♦ Write a brief letter to a Catholic friend, explaining the truth about Mary.

♦ Write a short prayer in the space below thanking the Lord Jesus for being your redeemer, mediator, and advocate with the Father. Pledge your love to Him, and give Him your wholehearted devotion.

Chapter 11

The Truth About Apparitions

*I*n January, 1995, I visited a Marian exhibit on the fifth floor of a huge mall in Metro Manila, Philippines. There were some twenty-five statues of Mary, representing different apparitions from Lourdes, Fatima, Guadalupe in Mexico, and many other places.

Crowds of people were placing their written wishes near one or the other statue. It was interesting to listen in on various conversations. They talked about how powerful certain images were. I even heard some betting that their preferred image was more powerful than some other.

I saw a lady praying the Rosary in front of a small, black representation of an apparition somewhere in Africa. I approached her and started a conversation. She happened to be one of the sponsors and organizers of the exhibit, and one who helped distribute answers to the wishes of those who visited the exhibit. She seemed open to me, although somewhat reserved. I ventured asking her a question.

"Which of all these Marys represents the true mother of Jesus?"

Quite surprised, she answered: *"Of course, all of them!"*

"How many mothers did Jesus have?" I asked.

"Only one!" she replied.

"How is it then that some are white, others brown, still others are black?" I insisted.

"Because that is the way she was described by those who saw her in the different apparitions," she answered.

"Don't you think that if the Lady appearing is the true mother of Jesus, she would always be the same?" I continued.

"You should ask the priests!" was her final response.

She smiled and went to pray in front of the Lady of Perpetual Help.

Widespread Belief In
The Apparitions Of Mary

Catholics commonly go on pilgrimages, sometimes at great expense, visiting special places where Mary allegedly appeared. The shrines at Lourdes and Fatima are famous all over the world. Other popular apparition sites include: Garabandal, Guadalupe, Aparecide in Brazil, and Syracuse in Italy. The present Pope (Pope John Paul II) is a great devotee of "Our Lady of Cestochowa" in Poland.

This leads us to the question of apparitions and miracles attributed to Mary. Did Mary really appear from heaven? Did she really speak to those who claim to have heard her? Did she really work all those miracles that are attributed to her at Fatima and Lourdes and elsewhere?

We do not question whether or not Bernadette Soubirous in France, or the three seers in Fatima, or the old man in Guadalupe really saw a lady appearing to them. Neither do we question the miracles that allegedly took place in the shrine where the lady appeared.

But the real question is this: Is the lady which these people saw really Mary? Is she the one doing all these miracles?

The Problem Of A Deceiver

The Bible teaches that there is an enemy of our souls whose purpose is to lead people astray from the truth. He intends to deceive the world with lies.

> *The great dragon was hurled down—that ancient serpent called the devil, or Satan, who leads the whole world astray (Rev. 12:9a).*

In order to succeed in deceiving men, he does not appear for what he really is—as the ugly enemy of God, but rather "as an angel of light."

> *[13]For such men are false apostles, deceitful workmen, masquerading as apostles of Christ. [14]And no wonder, for Satan himself masquerades as an angel of light (2 Corinthians 11:13, 14).*

Satan can work miracles, and will use them to accomplish his purposes. In the book of Exodus, Moses did great miracles by God's power in order to convince Pharaoh to release the people of Israel from slavery to the Egyptians. But Pharaoh's magicians, deriving power from Satan, duplicated almost all the miracles of Moses in an attempt to harden Pharaoh's heart against the will of God.

In the New Testament, the Lord Jesus warned of false prophets who will perform miracles in order to lead believers astray:

> *Many false Christs and false prophets will appear and perform great signs and miracles to deceive even the elect —if that were possible (Matthew 24:24).*

Likewise, in the Old Testament God warns His people not to follow after false prophets who do miracles. He says that such prophets are allowed to do miracles in order to test our love for Him—to see if we will remain loyal or choose rather to follow after other wonder-working gods.

All sincere believers must consider the possibility that the one who appeared at places like Fatima and Lourdes was an impostor.

>¹*If a prophet, or one who foretells by dreams, appears among you and announces to you a miraculous sign or wonder,* [the words "sign" and "wonder" are the Old Testament equivalents of prophecy and miracle], ²*and if the sign or wonder of which he has spoken takes place, and he says, "Let us follow other gods . . . . and let us worship them,"* ³*you must not listen to the words of that prophet or dreamer. The LORD your God is testing you to find out whether you love him with all your heart and with all your soul* ⁴*It is the LORD your God you must follow, and him you must revere. Keep his commands and obey him; serve him and hold fast to him* (Deuteronomy 13:1-4).

Since such false prophets do exist, all believers need to be alert to the possibility of an impostor. How can we know an impostor from a true prophet of God? Both the impostor and the true prophet can do miracles; both appear to be good. The only way we can distinguish a false prophet from a true one is by comparing his message with the unchanging truths of the Gospel.

How can we distinguish a false prophet from a true one if both can do miracles?

The Word Of God, The Test Of Truth

The message of anyone who claims to speak for God can be accepted only after examination and comparison with the message of the apostles as recorded in the Word of God, the Bible.

The apostle Paul, after solemnly stating his credentials, writes to the church at Galatia:

> *But even if we or an angel from heaven should preach a gospel other than the one we preached to you, let him be eternally condemned (Galatians 1:8, NIV)!*

The Holy Spirit through the apostle Paul tells us that we should not even believe an angel from heaven, if what he says is contrary to the message of the Gospel. Such an angel cannot be from God: it is Satan disguised like an angel of light.

Jesus taught His followers to base their faith upon the Word of God, not upon miracles that people perform. He says:

> *22Many will say to me on that day, 'Lord, Lord, did we not prophesy in your name and in your name drive out demons and perform many miracles?' 23Then I will tell them plainly, 'I never knew you. Away from me, you evildoers!' 24Therefore everyone who hears these words of mine and puts them into practice is like a wise man who built his house on the rock. 25The rain came down, the streams rose, and the winds blew and beat against that house; yet it did not fall, because it had its foundation on the rock (Matthew 7:22-25).*

The words of Jesus are a solid rock. Those who build the edifice of their spiritual life on His Word will not be destroyed in the flood. Miracles and apparitions are like sand; they are not a good foundation upon

The message of anyone who claims to speak for God can be accepted only after examination and comparison with the message of the Word of God, the Bible.

which to build a life. Many who rely on miracles as proof of their relationship to God will hear the Lord say: "I never knew you. Away from me, you evildoers!" True believers trust Jesus Christ himself as a Person and believe and accept His words as revealed in the Scriptures.

♦   Which of the following is the most reliable test of truth?
    ____ Check to see if what the messenger says is backed up by signs and wonders (miracles).
    ____ Check to see if what the messenger says is consistent with the message of the Apostles as recorded in the Holy Scriptures.
    ____ Check to see if the messenger claims to be from God.
    ____ Check to see if the messenger can drive out demons.

Who Really Appeared, Mary Or An Impostor?

In October, 1917, something miraculous took place at Fatima, a small town in Portugal. According to eyewitnesses, thousands of people watched as "the sun whirled in the sky, then seemed to tear itself from the heavens and come crashing down upon the horrified multitude. Just when it seemed the ball of fire would fall upon and destroy them the miracle ceased."

This occasion marked the end of a series of appearances, first by an angel, then by a woman who claimed to be "the Lady of the Rosary" to three young children. No one else saw the lady. The miracle was to be a sign that would confirm to observers that she really was appearing to the children with a message she claimed was "from heaven."

While some would never dare to ask, "Who really appeared to the children, Mary, or an impostor?" the question must be asked in the interest of truth. The fact that she brought down a "ball of fire" from heaven proves nothing. The Bible specifically states that a false prophet in the last days will cause *fire to come down from heaven to earth in full view of man* in order to commend worship of the antichrist (Revelation 13:13). The only way to know the answer to this question we have dared ask is to compare the revelations of the "Lady of the Rosary" with the message of the apostles as recorded in the Word of God.

♦   What kind of miracle does the Bible say the false prophet in the last times will do in order to commend worship of the antichrist (Revelation 13:13)?

♦   What kind of miracle was done at Fatima?

♦   What can we learn from these facts?
    ____   It is possible that the person who appeared at Fatima is not from God.
    ____   The person who appeared at Fatima was without a doubt from God.

♦   Apply the surest test of truth. On the left of pages 164 to 167 are messages of the lady. On the right, words of the apostles. I have underlined certain phrases in order to highlight the contrasts between the two. Study the chart below and compare the message of the lady with the message of Scripture to see if what the lady said is true.

Message of the Lady	Word of God, the Bible
"God ... wishes to establish throughout the world <u>devotion to my Immaculate heart</u>. To all who embrace it, I promise salvation" (2nd Apparition, June 13, 1917).	"But I am afraid that just as Eve was deceived by the serpent's cunning, your minds may somehow be led astray from pure and sincere <u>devotion to Christ</u>. For if someone comes to you and preaches a Jesus other than the Jesus we preached, or if you receive a different spirit from the one you received, or a different gospel from the one you accepted, you put up with it easily enough" (2 Corinthians 11:3, 4).
"<u>My Immaculate heart</u> will be your refuge and <u>the way</u> that will lead you to God" (2nd Apparition, June 13, 1917).	"<u>Jesus</u> answered, <u>I am the way</u>, the truth, and the life. No one comes to the Father except through me" (John 14:6).
"Pray, pray very much, and make sacrifices for sinners, for many souls go to hell because there was <u>nobody to make sacrifices</u> and pray for them" (3rd Apparition, July 13, 1917).	"We have been made holy through the sacrifice of the body of Jesus once for all .... When this priest had offered for all time one sacrifice for sins, he sat down at the right hand of God ... because <u>by one sacrifice he has made perfect forever</u> those who are being made holy" (Hebrews 10: 10-13).
"You have seen hell where the souls of sinners go. <u>To save them</u> God wishes to establish devotion to <u>my Immaculate heart</u>" (3rd Apparition, July 13, 1917).	"For God so loved the world that He gave His one and only Son that <u>whoever believes in Him shall not perish</u> but have eternal life ... Whoever believes in the Son has eternal life, but whoever rejects the Son will not see life, for God's wrath remains on Him" (John 3:16, 36).

Message of the Lady	Word of God, the Bible
"I am the Lady of the Rosary. Continue to <u>pray the rosary</u> every day <u>so that God may forgive you</u> for your sins and that you may go to heaven" (6th Apparition, October 13, 1917).	"<u>Everyone who believes in Him (Jesus) receives forgiveness of sins</u> through His name" (Acts 10:43).

Here the lady urges people everywhere to pray the Rosary, a prayer addressed to Mary that we have already shown to be inappropriate on the lips of true believers. Worse still, she urges people to offer this prayer as payment for sin. This strikes at the very heart of the Gospel. Jesus Christ paid for our sins in full. Nowhere does the Bible teach that we have to do penance to receive forgiveness of sins. Jesus has already obtained forgiveness for all who trust in Him:

> *[1]My dear children, I write this to you so that you will not sin. But if anybody does sin, we have one who speaks to the Father in our defense—Jesus Christ, the Righteous One. [2]He is the atoning sacrifice* [the full payment] *for our sins, and not only for ours but also for the sins of the whole world (1 John 2:1, 2).*

Message of the Lady	Word of God, the Bible
"All those who during five months on the first Saturday shall confess, receive holy communion, pray five decades of the Rosary, and keep me company for fifteen minutes . . . I promise to assist them at the hour of death with all the <u>graces necessary for the salvation</u> of these souls" (Apparition in Pontevedra).	"Believe in the Lord Jesus and <u>you will be saved</u> . . ." (Acts 16:31).

Here the lady blatantly promises salvation to those who do certain things on the first Saturday of five consecutive months!

This same lady has appeared to others in such places as Guadalupe, Paris, La Sallette, Lourdes, Knock, Beauraing, and Banneux. Her message was the same.

Message of the Lady	Word of God, the Bible
In Paris, 1830, she said of the rays of light radiating from the rings on her fingers, "they are the graces I shed upon those who ask for them."	"Every good and perfect gift is from above, coming down from the Father of lights" (James 1:17).
At La Sallette, 1846, she said, "If my people will not obey, I shall be compelled to loose my Son's [Jesus'] arm. It is so heavy, so pressing, that I can no longer restrain it. How long I have suffered for you . . . ."	"Here is a trustworthy saying that deserves full acceptance: Christ Jesus came into the world to save sinners—of whom I am the worst. I was shown mercy so that in me, the worst of sinners, Christ Jesus might display His unlimited patience as an example for those who would believe on him and receive eternal life" (1 Timothy 1:15, 16).

Note that in the above word picture, the woman portrays Jesus as the one ready to destroy us, and she herself as the Savior. Thus, she steals our affections away from Jesus and focuses them on herself.

Message of the Lady	Word of God, the Bible
To Saint Simon Stock, in 1251, she said: "Whoever dies clothed in this [the scapular], shall never suffer eternal fire."	"Whoever believes in Him [Jesus] is not condemned, but whoever does not believe stands condemned already because he has not believed in the name of God's one and only Son" (John 3:18).

We may have a scapular around our necks, but if we do not have Jesus in our hearts, we are condemned already. Salvation belongs to those who believe in Christ, not to those who wear this lady's medallion. Such superstitions have turned the faith of many away from Christ and caused them to trust in pieces of cloth and metal.

Message of the Lady	Word of God, the Bible
"I want to tell you that a chapel [shrine] is to be built here in my honor. I am the Lady of the Rosary. Continue always to pray the Rosary every day" (Sixth Apparition, October 17, 1917).	"You shall not make for yourself an idol in the form of anything in heaven above or on the earth beneath or in the waters below" (Exodus 20:3).

Many other quotes could be cited, but those cited above are sufficient to determine whether or not this lady is Mary, the mother of Jesus, sent by God.

♦ Read the following verses carefully.

> *But I am afraid that just as Eve was deceived by the serpent's cunning, your minds may somehow be led astray from your sincere and pure devotion to Christ (2 Corinthians 11:3).*

♦ The verse quoted above from the Bible says that Satan wants to lead people astray from sincere and pure devotion to Christ. Did the lady who appeared above inspire pure devotion to Christ or did she distract from it?

    ____ Yes, she urged devotion to Christ alone and to no one else.

    ____ No, because she urged devotion to herself and to her own "immaculate heart."

♦   Read the following verses carefully.

> *⁶I am astonished that you are so quickly deserting the one who called you by the grace of Christ and are turning to a different gospel—⁷which is really no gospel at all. Evidently some people are throwing you into confusion and are trying to pervert the gospel of Christ. ⁸But even if we or an angel from heaven should preach a gospel other than the one we preached to you, let him be eternally condemned (Galatians 1:6-8)!*

♦   Paul rebuked the Galatian believers, warning them not to believe those who pervert the Gospel of Christ. In which of the following ways do you think the lady of the apparitions perverted the Gospel of Christ? Check those statements which you find to be true.

_____ She did not pervert the Gospel. She clearly taught the Gospel of salvation by faith in Christ alone.

_____ She perverted the Gospel by promising salvation to those who would be devoted to her.

_____ She perverted the Gospel by teaching that those who die clothed in the scapular shall never suffer eternal fire.

_____ She perverted the Gospel by asking people to pray the Rosary so that God might forgive their sins.

_____ She perverted the Gospel by claiming to be a mediator who gives grace to those who ask her for it.

_____ She perverted the Gospel by presenting herself as more merciful than the Lord Jesus.

_____ She perverted the Gospel by teaching that the sacrifice of Christ is not sufficient to pay for sins, but that further reparation (penance, the Rosary, etc.) is needed.

♦ What is Satan's purpose according to Revelation 12:9?

♦ How does Satan masquerade in his attempt to deceive (2 Corinthians 11:13,14)?

♦ Cite one example from the Old Testament that proves Satan will use miracles to deceive people.

♦ Cite one example from the New Testament that proves Satan will use miracles to deceive people.

♦ Is the message of Fatima consistent with the message of the apostles as recorded in the Bible?

♦ Who do you think appeared to those children, and why?

Chapter 12

The Truth About The Pope Part I

*A*s a young Catholic boy at home and in the Church, I developed great admiration and deep veneration for the Pope. I learned to cherish him in my heart and mind as the infallible head of the church, the "Vicar of Christ" on earth, and successor of the apostle Peter.

When I entered the seminary, they constantly preached to us about the three great loves all priests must have: the Eucharist (mass and communion), Mary, *and the Pope.*

As I started graduate studies, I was deeply disturbed by the contrast between what I learned about the Popes in church history, and what was taught in Systematic Theology. In Systematic Theology, the professor tried to prove that the Pope truly is the successor of Peter and "Vicar of Christ" on earth and that he should be respected and obeyed as such. He argued from history, tradition, the official magisterium of the Church, and even from the Bible. The Pope was esteemed as the infallible ruler and teacher of the church, not to mention lord over all earthly kings and emperors.

In my Church history classes, I learned about all the atrocities, vendettas, violence, worldliness, immoralities, riches, dishonesty and political intrigues of several Popes, especially during the Middle Ages and the Renaissance. While honestly teaching these facts of history, the professor was careful to reassure us that such sins did not in the least affect the truth of the Pope's infallibility as head of the Church!

I sincerely tried to understand and believe it, but in my heart I found it extremely hard to accept.

Roman Catholic Teaching About The Pope From Systematic Theology

In considering this all-important doctrine of the papacy, as with other major Catholic doctrines, we will only concern ourselves with the teaching of the Church as contained in the dogmatic definitions, the official documents of the ecumenical councils, and the teachings of the Popes. These represent the actual teaching of the Church, regardless of what some Catholics believe, what certain priests teach today, or even what some bishops may have written. The following statements are all duly documented.

The acceptance of the authority of the Pope and submission to him is necessary for salvation!

> *Furthermore We declare, state and define [dogmatic statement] that it is absolutely necessary for the salvation of all men that they submit to the Roman Pontiff.*[1]

---

[1]Bull Unam Sanctum of Pope Boniface VIII, 1302. *The Teaching of The Catholic Church*, by Neuner and Roos, S.J. p. 204, No. 342.

The Primacy Of The Pope

We decree that the Holy Apostolic See and the Roman Pontiff have primacy in the whole world, and that this Roman Pontiff is the successor of blessed Peter, the Prince of the Apostles, and true "Vicar of Christ," head of the whole Church and father and teacher of all Christians; that to him in blessed Peter was given by our Lord Jesus Christ the full power of feeding, ruling and governing the universal Church as it is contained in the acts of the ecumenical councils and in the sacred canons.[2]

If any one, therefore, shall say that blessed Peter the Apostle was not appointed the Prince of all the Apostles and the visible head of the whole Church; or that he directly and immediately received a primacy of honor only, and not of true and proper jurisdiction [right of power over] — let him be anathema [excommunicated and condemned].[3]

Hence We teach and declare that by the appointment of our Lord the Roman Church possesses a superiority of ordinary power over all other Churches, and that this power of jurisdiction of the Roman Pontiff, which is truly Episcopal, is immediate; to which all, of whatever rite or dignity, both pastors and faithful, both individually and collectively, are bound by their duty of hierarchical subordination and true obedience, to submit, not only in matters that pertain to faith and morals, but also in those that pertain to discipline and government of the Church throughout the world.[4]

If then any one shall say that the Roman Pontiff has merely the office of inspection and direction, but not full

---

[2]Council of Florence, 1439. Ibid., p. 206, No. 349.
[3]Vatican Council I, 1870. Ibid., p. 223, No. 374.
[4]Ibid., pp. 224-225, No. 379.

and supreme power of jurisdiction over the universal Church, not only in things pertaining to faith and morals, but also in those things that relate to the discipline and government of the Church spread throughout the world; or that he possesses only the principal part, and not all the fullness of this supreme power ... Let him be excommunicated and condemned![5]

Many more quotations could be given from papal decrees, councils and dogmatic statements. But let me just give the text of the dogma of papal infallibility defined by Pope Pius IX in 1870 at the first Vatican Ecumenical Council:

Therefore, faithfully adhering to the tradition received from the beginning of the Christian faith, for the glory of God our Savior, the exaltation of the Catholic religion, and the salvation of Christian peoples, the sacred Council approving, We teach and define that it is a dogma divinely revealed: that the Roman Pontiff, when He speaks ex cathedra, that is, when in discharge of the office of Pastor and Doctor of all Christians, by virtue of His supreme apostolic authority He defines a doctrine regarding faith or morals to be held by the Universal Church, by the divine assistance promised him in blessed Peter, is possessed with that infallibility with which the Divine Redeemer willed that His church should be endowed for defining doctrine regarding faith or morals: and that therefore such definitions of the Roman Pontiff are irreformable of themselves, and not from the consent of the Church. But if any one—which God avert—presume to contradict this Our definition—Let him be excommunicated and condemned![6]

---

[5]Vatican Council I. Ibid., p. 226, No. 382.
[6]Ibid., p. 229, No. 388.

Catholic Statements About The Pope

The Pope is usually and formally addressed as: *Most Holy Father.*[7]

In the Cardinals' Oath, Pope Pius X is addressed as: *Our Most Holy Lord.*[8]

The famous historian Moreri writes: *To make war against the Pope is to make war against God.*[9]

The writer Decius states: *The Pope can do all things God can do.*[10]

What Popes Say Of Themselves[11]

Leo XIII (1902) said:

> *The supreme teacher in the Church is the Roman Pontiff. Union of minds, therefore, requires, together with a perfect accord in the one faith, complete submission and obedience of will to the Church and to the Roman Pontiff, as to God Himself.*[12]

Pope Pius X stated:

> *The Pope is not only the representative of Jesus Christ, but He is Jesus Christ Himself hidden under the veil of flesh. Does the Pope speak? It is Jesus Christ who speaks.*[13]

---

[7]See encyclical by Leo XIII as introduction to the Douay version of the Bible.
[8]From the Article *"Scriptures For Roman Catholics,"* by Dr. Bartholomew Brewer.
[9]Ibid.
[10]Ibid.
[11]Ibid.
[12]Ibid.
[13]Ibid.

Pope Pius XI once declared:

> *You know that I am the Holy Father, the representative of God on earth, the Vicar of Christ, which means that I am God on the earth.*[14]

Consider the contrast between the above statements about the Pope and Peter, and what the Word of God says:

What the Popes say about themselves	What the first apostles said:
"Union of minds requires . . . submission and obedience . . . to the Roman Pontiff, as to God Himself" (Leo XIII).	"To the elders among you I appeal as a fellow elder" (The apostle Peter in 1 Peter 5:1). "Be shepherds of God's flock that is under your care, serving . . . not lording it over those entrusted to you, but being examples" (The apostle Peter to other bishops in 1 Peter 5:3).
"The Pope . . . is Jesus Christ himself, hidden under the veil of flesh" (Pope Pius X).	"Men, why are you doing this [offering sacrifices to Paul, Barnabas, and the apostles]? We too are only men, human like you . . ." (Acts 14:14, 15).
"I am God on the earth" (Pope Piux XI).	"As Peter entered the house, Cornelius met him and fell at his feet in reverence. But Peter made him get up. 'Stand up,' he said, 'I am only a man.' " (Acts 10:25, 26)
The Pope is addressed as "Our Most Holy Father."	"And do not call anyone on earth 'father,' for you have one father, and He is in heaven" (*Jesus Christ* in Matthew 23:9).

---

[14]Ibid.

In the light of the holy Scriptures, certain dogmatic definitions and statements on the Pope sound quite blasphemous!

♦ How are the statements by the Popes mentioned on page 175 different from the statements of Peter about himself?

♦ Write a brief response to this statement: "It appears from a study of Scripture that the Popes have claimed powers for themselves that Peter never claimed for himself."

Troublesome Facts About The Personal Lives Of Certain Popes (Thoughts From Church History)

The stated dogmatic doctrines and beliefs about the Popes as Christ on earth, "Vicar of Christ," "Infallible Teacher," "Holy Father," "Most Holy Lord," and "Prince of the Apostles," are not only in open contrast with Scriptures, but even with history!

How could anyone, for example, refer to Pope Alexander VI (Alejandro Borja, a Spaniard who reigned in the 15th century) as "Most Holy" anything. He is well known for his lusty life and his cruelty! The Vatican was a harem of prostitutes during his reign. Pope Alexander VI kept his nephew (Cesar Borja, the Prince of Florence) on the throne by having Cesar's political rival killed in front of him on the staircase of St. Peter's Basilica.

Even Catholic historians admit the wickedness of certain Popes. The following excerpts were taken from *The Catholic Encyclopedia*:

About Boniface VII:

> *He overpowered John XIV and thrust him into the dungeons of Sant'Angelo, where the wretched man died*

four months later ... for more than a year Rome endured this <u>monster</u> steeped in the blood of his predecessors.[15] [Emphasis mine].

About Boniface VIII:

Scarcely any possible crime was omitted: infidelity, heresy, simony, gross and unnatural immorality [homosexuality], magic [sorcery] ... Protestant historians generally, and even modern Catholic writers, class him among the wicked Popes. An ambitious, haughty and unrelenting man, deceitful also and treacherous, his whole pontificate was one record of evil![16]

History tells us how he reduced his political enemies to dire poverty and misery by having their fields sown with salt, so that they might not produce anything for years! No wonder the Italian poet *Dante Alighieri* in his *Divine Comedy* places Boniface the VIII in hell!

About John XI we read:

Some, taking Bishop Liutprand of Cremona and the "Liber Pontiicalis" as their authority, assert that he was the natural [illegitimate] son of Pope Sergius III. Through the intrigues of his mother who ruled in Rome at that time, he was raised to the chair of Peter.[17]

About John XII:

A coarse, immoral man, whose life was such that the Lateran [his residence and main Church] was spoken of as a brothel, and the moral corruption in Rome became the subject of general odium [hatred] ... On November 6th a synod composed of fifty Italian and German bishops

---

[15] *The Catholic Encyclopedia*, Vol. 2, p. 661-662.
[16] Ibid., Vol. 2, p. 668.
[17] Ibid., Vol. 1, p. 426.

convened in St. Peter's. John XII was accused of sacrilege, simony, perjury, murder, adultery and incest.[18]

Generally, Roman Catholic theologians and priests, when confronted with these undeniable facts, respond that this is a proof that the Catholic Church is the one true Church, having survived in spite of so many evil Popes! But such an answer does not in the least solve the problem of how such Popes could be considered and called "Holy," "Christs on Earth," "Infallible," "Teachers," "Most Holy Lords," "Heads of Christ's Church"!

Many Catholics will object that even Evangelical leaders fall into sin. We admit that, but there are two big differences!

1. No Evangelical leader ever claimed to be the infallible "Vicar of Christ" and head of the Church!

2. Evangelical leaders who fall into scandalous sin or basic theological error are either disciplined by their church or exposed as false teachers!

But the Church of Rome always tries to hide the sins and errors of its Popes, bishops and priests. When it cannot do so, in the case of the Popes especially, it either tries to deny the evidence or to defend their status and authority in spite of the facts. So we have the horrible situation of public, scandalous sinners, dishonest and immoral Popes and bishops, who continued to hold their post of power and authority simply because they are recognized as *Vicars of Christ* and successors of the apostles! One can find no support in the Bible for such aberration!

♦ Read the following qualifications for being an overseer (bishop) as recorded in God's Word.

> *[1]Here is a trustworthy saying: If anyone sets his heart on being an overseer, he desires a noble task. [2]Now the overseer must be above reproach, the husband of but one*

---

[18]Ibid., Vol. VIII, p. 427.

wife, temperate, self-controlled, respectable, hospitable, able to teach, ³not given to drunkenness, not violent but gentle, not quarrelsome, not a lover of money. ⁴He must manage his own family well and see that his children obey him with proper respect. ⁵(If anyone does not know how to manage his own family, how can he take care of God's church?) ⁶He must not be a recent convert, or he may become conceited and fall under the same judgment as the devil. ⁷He must also have a good reputation with outsiders, so that he will not fall into disgrace and into the devil's trap (1 Timothy 3:1-7).

Claims Of The Papacy Disproved
From The Scriptures

Catholic theology, recognizing the total silence about the papacy in the Bible, concentrates its efforts on Peter, who is considered the Prince of the apostles. I regard this a very subtle deception! Most Catholics take it for granted that the Pope is the legitimate successor of the apostle Peter! Yet, there is no biblical or historical proof for it! More than that, from God's Word we can prove that there is no connection between Peter and the founder of the Church of Rome. So even if what the Catholic Church teaches about Peter were true, this absolutely could not be attributed to the Pope! Nevertheless, I want to show that the Catholic doctrine about Peter himself is not biblical.

The Catholic Church uses Matthew 16:18-19 to prove its doctrine about Peter as head of the Church and infallible "Vicar of Christ":

¹⁸And I tell you that you are Peter, and on this rock I will build my church, and the gates of Hades will not overcome it. ¹⁹I will give you the keys of the kingdom of heaven; whatever you bind on earth will be bound in

*heaven, and whatever you loose on earth will be loosed
in heaven.*

From these two verses Catholicism derives the following
teachings:

1. Peter was made the "Vicar of Christ" and head of the
    Church (Upon this rock . . .).
2. Peter was declared infallible (". . . the gates of Hades
    will not prevail . . .").
3. Peter was given all power ("I give you the keys . . .").

♦   What Scripture passage does the Catholic Church use to
    prove its doctrine that Peter is the "Vicar of Christ" and
    the infallible "Head of the Church"?

♦   What three teachings does the Roman Catholic Church
    derive from these verses?

In the next section we will examine the text and context
of Matthew 16:18-19 to determine if these verses really teach
what the Catholic Church claims.

Did Jesus Make Peter The Vicar Of Christ And The Head Of The Church?

The first teaching the Catholic Church claims to derive from
this passage comes from the statement: ". . . upon this rock I
will build my church." They claim that by these words Jesus
made Peter the vicar of Christ and the head of the Church.

Jesus had been teaching in public for more than a year.
In the verses preceding those quoted above, Jesus conducts a
little evaluation. He asks his disciples what people are thinking

about Him. What kind of rumors are going around? (*Who do people say the Son of Man is?*) His disciples replied:

> *Some say John the Baptist; others say Elijah; and still others Jeremiah or one of the prophets (Matthew 16:14).*

Jesus may have found some consolation in the fact that the people did recognize which team He was on. However, they still did not understand who He was and what position He played.

What about the disciples? Did they understand? Jesus asked them point blank:

> *"But what about you?" He asked. "Who do you say I am?" (Matthew 16:15).*

It was Peter who spoke first:

> *You are the Christ, the Son of the living God.*

Jesus was pleased with Peter's answer. The people did not yet understand. But Peter did. Peter was the first among the disciples to publicly confess that Jesus is Savior (Messiah) and Lord (the Son of the Living God)!

Delighted with Peter's profession of faith, Jesus proceeded to bless Peter and to announce the founding of His Church.

> *[17]Jesus replied, "Blessed are you, Simon son of Jonah, for this was not revealed to you by man, but by my Father in heaven. [18]And I tell you that you are Peter, and on this rock I will build my church, and the gates of Hades will not overcome it. [19]I will give you the keys of the kingdom of heaven; whatever you bind on earth will be bound in heaven, and whatever you loose on earth will be loosed in heaven" (Matthew 16:17-19).*

♦ What confession did Peter make that was the occasion for this blessing?

You are the _____, the _____ of the Living God.

In blessing Peter, Jesus used two figures of speech. (1) He spoke of the church as a building ("I will build my church"). And, (2) he spoke of a rock (*petra*) as one of the building blocks that make up the church building. Some argue that *petra* is not the same as *petros*. In context, however, *Petra* does refer to Peter, not the unregenerate Simon, but the believing *Petros* (Peter), the first "living stone" in the building of the church. The difference between "Simon" and "Peter" is faith. We, like Peter, become living stones when we believe in Jesus. Peter himself says so in his first epistle:

> [4]*As you come to him, the living stone—rejected by men but chosen by God and precious to him—*[5]*you also, like living stones, are being built into a spiritual house . . . (1 Peter 2:4, 5).*

The Church of Christ would be a community of people like Peter, who truly accept Jesus as their Savior and Lord! As the apostle Paul says in his letter to the Romans:

> [9]*That if you confess with your mouth "Jesus is Lord," and believe in your heart that God raised him from the dead, you will be saved.* [10]*For it is with your heart that you believe and are justified, and it is with your mouth that you confess and are saved (Romans 10:9, 10).*

Peter, being the first to publicly confess Christ, would be the first stone placed in the foundation of the building. He would soon be joined by the other apostles and disciples!

> [19]*Consequently, you are no longer foreigners and aliens, but fellow citizens with God's people and members of God's household [the Church],* [20]*built on the foundation of the apostles and prophets, with Christ Jesus Himself as the chief cornerstone (Ephesians 2:19-20).*

Faith is the only requirement to be a living stone of the Church (1 Peter 2:5). Faith comes by hearing the Word of Christ (Romans 10:12-17). Therefore, the prophets who announced the

Messiah and the apostles who proclaimed Him are the foundation upon which the church is built (Ephesians 2:19, 20). Through their word we come to know Him, and by knowing Him we can believe and be members of His Church.

> *[12]For there is no difference between Jew and Gentile—the same Lord is Lord of all and richly blesses all who call on him, [13]for, "Everyone who calls on the name of the Lord will be saved." [14]How, then, can they call on the one they have not believed in? [15]And how can they believe in the one of whom they have not heard? And how can they hear without someone preaching to them? And how can they preach unless they are sent? As it is written, "How beautiful are the feet of those who bring good news!" [16]But not all the Israelites accepted the good news. For Isaiah says, "Lord, who has believed our message?" [17]Consequently, faith comes from hearing the message, and the message is heard through the word of Christ (Romans 10:12-17).*

Important Information:

On Matthew 16:18, the "Peter-Rock controversy," Archbishop Kenrick of St. Louis, USA, brought to the Vatican Council I in 1870 a speech, which was not delivered or published, on the five "Patristic Interpretations":[19]

1. 17 Church Fathers understood the rock to be Peter.
2. 8 understood the rock to be the Apostles.
3. 44 say that the rock is Peter's confession of Faith in Christ (among them Origen and Chrysostom).

---

[19]Quoted by W.H. Griffith Thomas, *Principles of Theology,"* 1930, pp. 470-471.
John R.W. Stott, *Understanding Christ,* (Zondervan Publishing House, Grand Rapids, Michigan, 1981), p. 49.

4. 16 (including Augustine, Jerome, and Gregory the Great) interpret the rock to be Jesus Christ Himself.
5. For few the rock would mean the faithful in general.

The majority of the Fathers held that the rock should be understood as "THE FAITH PROFESSED BY PETER," not "PETER PROFESSING THE FAITH."

Did Jesus Declare Peter To Be An Infallible Teacher?

The second teaching the Catholic Church claims to derive from this passage comes from the statement: "the gates of Hades will not overcome it." Roman Catholics interpret this to mean that "Peter and his successors," the Popes, cannot err. This is obviously a faulty interpretation. Jesus specifically said "the gates of Hades will not overcome *it*," not "you," referring to the *Church*, not Peter. With these words Jesus did not promise that "Peter and his successors" would be infallible, but that His Church would be indefectible. Christ's Church will never disappear. It will never be overcome by death!

Did Jesus Give Peter Absolute Power To Rule In The Church?

The third teaching Catholicism claims to derive from this passage is that Peter has all power. They take this from the phrase "I will give you the keys of the kingdom . . . ." They argue that the word "keys" means absolute power.

Both Catholics and Evangelical Christians understand the word "key" is being used figuratively. What does it stand for? Keys are used to open and close. The context indicates the "key" represents the authority to open and close. Was Peter given the authority to open and close the gates of the kingdom allowing some to enter, while forbidding others?

The Scriptures plainly teach that *faith is the key* that opens the door to heaven. Certainly the giving of "the keys" does not imply that Peter has the authority to open the gates of heaven to an unbeliever or to close them to a believer. The authority that Jesus gave to Peter was the authority to open the doors of heaven **through the preaching of the Gospel.** The gates of heaven are open to a person when he or she believes. They cannot believe, however, unless someone preaches to them:

> *Faith comes from hearing the message, and the message is heard through the word of Christ (Romans 10:17).*

Jesus gave these same keys (authority to bind and loose, to preach the Gospel) to all the disciples in Matthew 18:18 and Matthew 28:19-21. Peter was granted the greatest of all privileges and tasks, that of *sharing Christ and His Word with all people.*

The word key is used by Jesus Himself in reference to the knowledge of the truth:

> *Woe to you, experts in the law, because you have taken away the key to knowledge. You yourselves have not entered, and you have hindered those who were entering (Luke 11:52).*

Understandably, Roman Catholics will object: "How sure can you be that this is what the Bible teaches, and not rather how the Pope interprets it?"

The answer is simple. Peter himself interprets what was given to him by his words and ministry in the book of Acts, as well as in his two epistles. He understood what Jesus meant and implemented it. In the next chapter, we will study his life and ministry as recorded in the infallible Scriptures.

♦ What is the key that opens the door to heaven?

♦ In what way was Peter given the key to open the door of heaven to others?

Conclusion

♦ According to the dogmas of the Catholic Church, how important is it for a person to submit to the Roman Pontiff (see p. 171)?

It is absolutely _____ for the salvation of all men.

♦ What do the canons say about the Pope's authority (see p. 172)?

He is the ____ of the whole Church, the father and _____ of all Christians.

♦ What did the first Vatican Ecumenical Council conclude about the Pope when he speaks ex cathedra (see p. 173)?

He is possessed with _____.

♦ What did Pope Alexander VI do to keep his nephew on the throne in Florence (see p. 176)?

♦ Why is Boniface VIII classified as one of the "wicked Popes" (see p. 177)?

♦ How did Pope John XI rise to the chair of Peter (see p. 178)?

◆ Of what was John XII accused at the November 6 synod (see p. 177)?

◆ According to the Word of God, what qualifies a person to hold the office of bishop (see pp. 178-179)?
    ____ His godly life and character
    ____ His unquestionable authority as head of the church

◆ What two figures of speech did Jesus use in blessing Peter (see p. 182)?
    1. He spoke of the Church as a _____.
    2. He spoke of Peter as a _____, the first building block placed in the foundation of the building.

◆ Peter was not the whole foundation, but only a part of it. According to Ephesians 2:19-20, of what does the Church's foundation consist (see p. 182)?

◆ Who is the chief cornerstone (see p. 182)?

◆ Peter became a "living stone" when he confessed Jesus as Lord and Savior. According to 1 Peter 2:4,5, who else are "living stones" in the Church (see p. 182)?

◆ How does a person become a living stone (see p. 182)?

♦ How do Roman Catholics interpret the phrase "the gates
   of Hades will not overcome it" (see p. 184)?
   ____ They interpret it to mean that Peter and his
           successors are infallible.
   ____ They interpret it to mean that the Church of Christ
           is indefectible.

♦ Jesus said, "I will build my church, and the gates of Hades
   will not overcome it." To what does "it" refer (see p. 184)?
   ____ To the church
   ____ To Peter

♦ What do you think is the most accurate and honest
   interpretation of what Jesus said?
   ____ Peter and his successors are infallible.
   ____ The Church of Christ is indefectible.

Chapter 13

The Truth
About The Pope
Part II

As a student preparing for priesthood, I heard Matthew 16:18 quoted repeatedly by professors and preachers: *"You are Peter, and upon this rock I will build my Church."* This was especially true on the feast of Saints Peter and Paul, celebrated on the twenty-ninth of June.

One day, as the professor was explaining the meaning of that verse, my eyes went ahead in the text to verse 23 where Jesus said to Peter, *"Get behind me, Satan! You are a stumbling block to me; you do not have in mind the things of God, but the things of men."* Here Jesus calls Peter, whom he allegedly had just appointed the infallible "Vicar of Christ" and head of the Church, both *Satan* and a *stumbling block* because he denied the necessity of Christ's death and resurrection. I really did not fully understand all the implications of Peter's denial at the time. Yet I truly felt there must have been something seriously wrong with his words and his attitude for Jesus to react that way and call him *Satan*. Not even Judas had been so treated by Jesus. I sensed that Peter's statements, besides showing great boldness, must have been a terrible blunder, definitely not in keeping with the infallibility attributed to the head of the Catholic Church.

Now, as a believer, I understand better the gravity of Peter's words, and Jesus' response. Peter, anticipating the kingdom and its glory, denied the necessity of the cross, and urged Jesus to avoid it. He enticed Jesus to establish the kingdom by some other way, just as Satan had done when He tempted Jesus in the wilderness at the beginning of Jesus' public ministry. Peter, the rock, became a stumbling block.

Jesus rebuked Peter, and then urged the disciples to enter with him by way of the cross: *If anyone would come after me, he must deny himself and take up his cross and follow me* (Matthew 16:24).

In the previous chapter, we studied Jesus' words to Peter in Matthew 16:18-19, giving careful attention to its historical and grammatical context. We concluded that Jesus did not confer to Peter the powers of the Pope. We will now test our conclusions by examining the ministry and words of Peter himself in the Holy Scriptures to see what he understood Jesus to mean by the statements in question. Did he see himself to be a Pope? Did he exercise the authority of a Pope? Did the other apostles consider him their Pope?

Did Peter Consider Himself To Be The Head Of The Church?

Peter never presented himself as the "Vicar of Christ" on earth nor as the head of the Church. Neither did the other apostles consider him such. The first Church council, which took place in Jerusalem, was not convened by Peter, but at the request of Paul. Even though Peter had a very important part in it and shared his convictions, it was James, the pastor of that church, who presided at the council, and summarized its conclusions (Acts 15:1-35).

Peter viewed himself as an apostle and a servant of Jesus Christ, with the same authority as the other apostles (1 Peter 1:1; 2 Peter 1:1; Ephesians 1:1; 1 Timothy 1:1). As a church leader, he introduced himself, not as the head of the Church, but simply as one among many elders, a fellow elder. He spoke to the other elders not as one with authority over them, but as one with them.[1]

> To the elders among you, *I appeal as a fellow elder*, a witness of Christ's sufferings and one who will share in the glory to be revealed (1 Peter 5:1). [Emphasis mine].

Unlike the Pope, who *is accountable to no human authority*,[2] Peter submitted to the authority of the Church. On one occasion he and John were *sent* by the apostles to Samaria (Acts 8:14).

♦ Are there examples in Scripture of Peter exercising authority over other apostles, or the church? (If so, list the references below.)

How Did Peter Use The 'Keys' That Were Given To Him?

In Jerusalem, Peter used the "keys" to open the doors of the kingdom of heaven to Jews from all over Asia, Africa, and Europe on the day of Pentecost. He preached the Gospel of

---

[1]Peter describes himself in 1 Peter 5:1 as συμπρεσβυτερος, a fellow elder or co-elder. He did not command his co-workers, but rather appealed to them (παρακαλω, literally to encourage).

[2]*The Teaching of the Catholic Church*, by Neuner & Roos, S.J., p. 226, No. 381.

Jesus Christ, His death and resurrection. He proclaimed the forgiveness of sins and salvation through faith in Christ alone (Acts 2:23-24). He taught the necessity of repentance and genuine conversion (Acts 2:38; 3:19).

Peter also *opened the door for the Gentiles* as he shared the same Gospel to Cornelius and his household (Acts 10).

The Catholic Church claims that along with the keys, Peter was given the authority to absolve sin. In the biblical record, there is no mention of such a practice. Peter did confront a sinner on one occasion and tell him how to find forgiveness. He did not say, "Confess your sins to me and I will absolve them." But rather, he said:

> *Repent of this wickedness and **pray to the Lord**. Perhaps he will forgive you for having such a thought in your heart (Acts 8:22) [Emphasis mine].*

Did Peter Consider Himself To Be The Church's One Infallible Teacher?

If Peter was appointed infallible head of the Church by the Lord Jesus, as alleged by the Catholic Church, then we would expect to find Peter behaving as such in the historical records of the New Testament (The Book of Acts). We would also expect to find clear teaching about this important "truth" in the Epistles. We see neither. We do see Peter relating to the other apostles, but never with any kind of superior power of jurisdiction. We do find a defense of the doctrines of our Christian faith, and warnings against false teachers, but never an appeal to Peter as the final authority on the matter.

As we study the life of the apostle Peter in the pages of the New Testament, we find, not an infallible Pope, but a fallible servant-leader (Matthew 16:21-26). In the second chapter of Paul's letter to the Galatians we find two important facts about the apostle Peter.

1. Peter was appointed by the early church as a missionary to the Jews.

Although Peter opened the doors of the kingdom of heaven for both Jews and Gentiles, as we saw in the Book of Acts, it was the apostle Paul who was called by God and sent by the Church of Antioch to evangelize the Gentiles. The twelve, including Peter, John and James, agreed that Peter should be a missionary to the Jews, and Paul to the Gentiles.

> *7On the contrary, they saw that I* [Paul] *had been entrusted with the task of preaching the gospel to the Gentiles, just as* **Peter** *had been to the Jews. 8For God, who was at work in the ministry of Peter as an apostle to the Jews, was also at work in my ministry as an apostle to the Gentiles. 9James, Peter and John . . . agreed that we should go to the Gentiles, and they to the Jews* (Galatians 2:7-9).

Based on the above statement of God's Word, Paul rather than Peter would have been the logical choice to head the Church at Rome. Rome was the capital of the Roman Empire; the center of the Gentile world! Paul (not Peter) was the one chosen to be the apostle to the Gentiles. Still today, more than 99% of Roman Catholic Church members are Gentiles, not Jews. If successors must be chosen, it should be Paul's successors, not Peter's, who head the Church of Rome. But, as it is, the only head of the true Church is the Lord Jesus Himself (Ephesians 5:23; Colossians 1:18)!

2. Peter was publicly rebuked by the apostle Paul for hypocrisy.

The apostle Paul publicly rebuked Peter for failing to be consistent in complying with the decisions of the Council of Jerusalem. Peter gave in to pressure from a certain group, and separated himself from Gentile Christians.

> [11] *When Peter came to Antioch, I opposed him to his face, because he was clearly in the wrong.* [12] *Before certain men came from James, he used to eat with the Gentiles. But when they arrived, he began to draw back and separate himself from the Gentiles because he was afraid of those who belonged to the circumcision group.* [13] *The other Jews joined him in his hypocrisy, so that by their hypocrisy even Barnabas was led astray (Galatians 2:11-13).*

This whole episode would never have occurred if Peter had been appointed by Jesus as the infallible head of the Church! Peter could not have been mistaken. Paul could not have rebuked him publicly.

♦ According to the following Bible verse, was this error by the apostle Peter a minor or a major offense?

> *When I saw that they were not acting in line with the truth of the gospel, I said to Peter in front of them all: "You are a Jew, yet you live like a Gentile and not like a Jew. How is it then, that you force Gentiles to follow Jewish customs?" (Galatians 2:14)*

_____ It is a major offense because Peter was not acting in line with truth.

_____ It is a major offense because Peter taught by his actions something contrary to the gospel.

_____ It is a major offense because Peter's actions caused division in the church.

_____ It is a minor offense. An "infallible teacher" can act out of line with the truth, and the "head of the church" can separate himself from believers of a different race or culture.

♦ What conclusion can you draw from a study of this encounter between Peter and Paul?

____ Peter was the infallible teacher and head of the Church and Paul respectfully submitted to his authority.

____ Peter was a fallible servant-leader as was the apostle Paul. They had equal authority. They both submitted to the decisions of the apostles at the Council at Jerusalem.

Was Peter The Bishop Of Rome?

The Catholic hierarchy is based upon the assumption that Peter was the founder of the Church of Rome, and its first bishop. His successors (the Popes) are those who fill his office as the bishop of that city.

The question needs to be asked: "Was Peter the founder and first bishop of the Church of Rome?" The Bible says nothing about Peter being in Rome. History, too, is silent. The Roman Catholic Church bases its claim on tradition.

The Claim That Peter Founded
The Church Of Rome And Served As Its Bishop
For More Than 20 Years Is Not Reliable Tradition

We can be fairly certain that Peter did visit Rome shortly before his alleged execution and the death of Paul. A letter to the Romans by Irenaeus (second century, 130 years after the death of the apostle) places Peter in Rome with Paul at this time.

However, as to the question of whether or not Peter was the founder and first bishop of Rome, there is nothing written until the fourth century. By this time the church had been infiltrated with many unbelievers because Constantine's successors declared "Christianity" the official religion of the Roman Empire.

Businessmen, politicians, teachers, and even the military were compelled to join Christianity. They joined, motivated more by fear than by faith. The leaders of this now institutionalized church were using every means to show that the Church of Rome had both divine and temporal power.

A clear example of this is the case of the alleged Donation of Constantine! This document has repeatedly been used by Popes and Councils to defend the temporal power of the Church of Rome. The purported document presumably certifies that Constantine donated properties to the Church and granted imperial power to the Pope. The document was supposedly found by Isidore, bishop of Seville, in Spain in the eighth century and was dated back to the time of Constantine in the fourth century! But, it is now proven and accepted by Catholic historians that this document was an eighth century forgery!!

We should not rely on oral tradition and religious documents written more than 300 years after the death of the apostles to prove a doctrine as fundamental as apostolic succession; especially when the true authority, God's Word, is totally silent.

The New Testament Records Contradict The Catholic Claim That Peter Was The Founder And Bishop Of Rome For More Than 20 Years.

The last of the New Testament books were written at the end of the first century by the apostle John. The entire New Testament was completed within thirty years *after* the death of Peter and fifty years *after* the alleged founding of the Church of Rome. While the New Testament says nothing about the presence of Peter in Rome, it says much about his life and ministry. The New Testament books of The Acts of the apostles and the Epistle to the Romans, accepted also by Catholics as inspired and inerrant, shed some light on the subject.

The Acts Of The Apostles

The Acts of the Apostles, the fifth book of the New Testament, gives a history of the early Church, including many of the activities of the apostles. Luke tells us that Peter was a leader at the church in Jerusalem. He preached on the day of Pentecost (Acts 2:14-42), performed notable miracles (Acts 3: 1-10; 5:12-26), disciplined offenders (Acts 5:1-11), defended the Gospel before the Sanhedrin (Acts 4:5-12), and traveled in Samaria (Acts 9:32-43). He was forced out of Jerusalem in AD 44 by Herod, but was back in Jerusalem by the time of the Jerusalem Council in AD 50 (Acts 12:1-19; 15:1-5). When the book of Corinthians was written (AD 55), Peter was traveling with his wife in Jewish evangelism (1 Corinthians 9:5).

In the last chapter of the book of Acts, Luke (Paul's traveling companion at the time) records the events of Paul's long awaited arrival in Rome (AD 61). The Church of Rome knew that this great apostle to the Gentiles was arriving. They made preparations and traveled a good distance to welcome him.

> *And so we came to Rome. The brothers there had heard that we were coming, and they traveled as far as the Forum of Appius and the Three Taverns to meet us (Acts 28:14-15).*

If Peter ("Head of the Church" and "Vicar of Christ" on earth) was in Rome at this time, certainly Paul would have visited him. It seems plausible that Peter might even have come to welcome this remarkable apostle and founder of churches himself. Moreover, if these things had taken place, surely they would have been historically significant enough that Luke, the accurate New Testament historian, would have noted them in his book. Yet there is absolutely no mention of Peter in the entire episode!

The Book Of Romans

We also have in the New Testament a letter to the Church
at Rome where Peter was supposed to have served as bishop
and "Vicar of Christ." This book was written between AD 56
and 58, several years before Peter's death. We might expect
to find in this book some hint of Peter's presence or influence
there. A search for Peter, however, in the book of Romans yields
nothing. The book is absolutely silent on the issue.

This letter was not merely to announce Paul's anticipated
arrival in Rome. It is the longest and most doctrinal of all Paul's
letters. With apostolic authority, Paul lays down basic doctrines
concerning salvation, holiness, faith, baptism, ethical principles
regarding Christian duties towards the family, the government
and the Church. It is almost inconceivable that an ordinary
apostle would even dare to write such a letter to the Christians
in Rome if their bishop was none less than the "Vicar of Christ"
on earth and the head of the whole Church!

As in all his epistles, Paul begins his letter to the Romans
by greeting the believers. He makes no mention of Peter! If
Peter had been there as bishop of that church or diocese, and
head of the universal Church, I would consider it highly
unethical of Paul not to mention him! This is especially true
when we consider the fact that in the last chapter of this letter
Paul mentions by name 26 different leaders and members of
the Church of Rome by name, but does not mention Peter.
There is no reference to Peter in the entire book. Does not
this silence speak very loudly to the fact that Peter was not
there?

When one reads the original Greek used by Paul, there
is another strong argument against the presence of Peter and
his authority in the Church of Rome. In the first chapter Paul
writes:

*I long to see you so that I may impart to you some
spiritual gift to make you strong (Romans 1:11).*

If Peter was the founder and bishop of the Church of Rome, what need would there be for Paul to come and strengthen it by imparting some spiritual gift?! What spiritual gift could the apostle Paul impart that Peter could not? If Peter was the bishop of Rome and the "Vicar of Christ" on earth, this statement by the apostle Paul is an insult to him. Peter certainly would have imparted the necessary gifts to the Church himself, if indeed he was their shepherd.

The expression "to make you strong" is better translated "that you may be established." The word "established" is a technical term used to describe a church that had enjoyed the presence and witness of one of the apostles. A New Testament church was considered truly established only when built on the foundation of the apostles and prophets (Ephesians 2:20). If the Church at Rome had Peter as their founder, what need would there be for the apostle Paul to come and "establish" it? These words, too, would have been an insult to Peter. By the year AD 58, the Church at Rome should have been considered the most established of all churches if indeed the Pope was their pastor!

Conclusion

Both Catholics and Evangelical Christians consider the canon of Scripture closed with the book of Revelation. The absolute silence of Holy Scriptures on the matter of Peter's presence in Rome as well as his authority as "Vicar of Christ" and head of the Church, should make all Catholics think well before blindly accepting these teachings of their church.

Adding to this silence of Scripture the various biblical and historical facts mentioned above, one cannot but conclude that Roman Catholic doctrines regarding the primacy of Peter and the infallible authority of the Pope as head of the universal Church have no foundation other than the Roman Catholic System of the Middle Ages.

Consider The Following

♦ Who presided at the first Church council and summarized its conclusions (Acts 15:1-35) (see pp. 190-191)?

♦ How does Peter relate to the other elders when writing to them concerning spiritual matters (1 Peter 5:1) (see p. 191)?

♦ How did Peter show submission to the Church and the other apostles in Jerusalem (Acts 8:14) (see p. 191)?

♦ How did Peter use the keys that Jesus gave him to open the doors of heaven to Jews from all over Asia on the Day of Pentecost (see pp. 191-192)?

♦ How did Peter use the keys to open the doors of heaven to the Gentiles (Acts 10) (see p. 192)?

♦ What did Peter tell Simon the Sorcerer (Acts 8:22) to do in order to receive forgiveness of sins (see p. 192)?

♦ Based on Galatians 2:11-13 (see p. 194):

What kind of error did Peter commit?

____ A practical wrongdoing

____ A doctrinal error

____ Both a practical error and a doctrinal error. It was a practical wrongdoing that was based on a doctrinal error.

If Peter were the infallible "Vicar of Christ," the head of the Church and the Prince of the apostles, do you think he would have done what he did?

____ Yes. Even infallible teachers can make mistakes.

____ No. Infallible teachers don't make mistakes like this.

How did Paul respond to Peter's error?

____ He rebuked him privately.

____ He rebuked him publicly.

____ He kept quiet so as to show proper respect to authority.

____ He recognized Peter to be infallible and did not question his actions.

If Peter had absolute authority, as the Catholic Church teaches he did, do you believe that Paul would have responded in the way he did?

____ Yes. Bishops today publicly reprimand the Pope to his face in matters involving ethics and doctrine.

____ No. Paul would have rebuked him privately or ignored the issue so as to show proper respect to the infallible teacher.

♦ How many years passed after the death of the apostles before it was recorded as tradition that Peter was the founder and first bishop of Rome (see p. 196)?

____ Less than 50 years

____ More than 100 years

____ More than 300 years

♦   Why are traditions dating from the fourth centuries onward unreliable (see p. 195)?

♦   When were the New Testament books written (see p. 196)?

♦   Why are the books of the New Testament more reliable than tradition?
    ____   Because they were all written in the first century when eye witnesses were still living
    ____   Because those who wrote were apostles and eye witnesses
    ____   Because they are inspired by God
    ____   All of the above

♦   What evidence is there that Peter's primary ministry focus was as an apostle to the Jews (Compare Galatians 2:7) (see p. 193)?

♦   What evidence seems to indicate that Peter was not in Rome, even as late as AD 61, when Paul first arrived there (see p. 197)?

♦   When did Paul write the letter to the Romans (see p. 198)?

♦   Peter died in AD 65-67. How many years before Peter died was the letter to the Romans written?

♦ What kind of letter is Romans (see p. 198)?

____ A short casual letter announcing his expected arrival

____ A long doctrinal letter to instruct the believers in Rome in the doctrines of salvation as well as practical Christian living

♦ Why did Paul want to go to Rome (Romans 1:11)?

♦ How many people are greeted by name in the closing salutation of Paul's letter to the Church at Rome (see p. 198)?

♦ Why do you think Paul wrote this doctrinal letter to the Church of Rome and did not mention Peter anywhere in it?

____ Because Paul was mad at Peter and wasn't speaking to him

____ Because Paul forgot the Pope was the pastor of the Church at Rome

____ Because the Church at Rome was not an established church, and Peter was not present there

____ Because Paul thought that Peter was incompetent to strengthen the Church of Rome himself

Chapter 14

The Truth About The Pope Part III

On June 3, 1963, my townmate Pope John XXIII died. As I read the news and details of the last moments of his life, I remember him repeatedly expressing a deep fear of death! He asked for prayers, because he was not sure about "God's inscrutable design"! The Pope, the Vicar of Christ, was afraid to die, because he was not sure where he would go! Now as a believer I realize why.

   On August 6, 1978, his successor Pope Paul VI also died. I was already an Evangelical missionary in the Philippines at the time. I still remember the Cardinal, Archbishop of Manila, repeatedly giving the sad announcement on television. Obviously it had been taped, because it was done with exactly the same words every hour on all channels. I jotted down his words, because they became very useful later on in Bible studies with Roman Catholics about the assurance of the true believer. Here is the substance of the Cardinal's words: "Dearly beloved, I am giving you the sad news of the departure of his holiness Pope Paul VI! Although we hope that by now he is enjoying that eternal life which he strove so hard to merit; nevertheless, not knowing the inscrutable plan of Almighty God, let us pray for his soul, that it may soon reach the well-deserved bliss!"

If the Pope is not sure, what about ordinary priests and bishops? What about ordinary Catholics? Jesus would never leave His own in such agony of uncertainty! How can the so-called head of the Church confirm and reassure others, if he himself is not sure?

Many Catholics, who were studying the Word of God as they heard the words of the Cardinal, were disillusioned with their religion and turned to Christ in faith.

History Contradicts Papal Infallibility

Before examining some of the theological blunders committed by Popes, I would like to go back to a period in the history of the Catholic Church that is known to historians as the Church's "Babylonian Captivity." Like the exile of Israel, it lasted almost 70 years.

For sixty-eight years (1309-1377), Popes had to reside in Avignon (France) instead of Rome. "Captivity" ended when Pope Gregory XI, tired of being controlled by the king of France, returned to Rome. Just when things seemed to be returning to normal, Pope Gregory died. His death initiated the darkest period in all the history of the papacy.

The Cardinals gathered immediately and elected an Italian Pope, Urban VI. This new Pope did not live up to their expectations, so they convened again and elected a French Pope, Clement VII. This newly elected Pope, realizing that the Romans did not like him, decided to return to France. The Cardinals sought to nullify the election of Urban VI, saying that they elected the Italian because they had been threatened by an Italian mob.

Urban VI (the Italian) did not recognize Clement VII (The Frenchman) and vice versa! Bishops, priests, theologians, and laity—even some who are now canonized saints in the Church of Rome—were divided in their allegiance! Whole countries took sides! France, Spain, Scotland and the kingdom of Naples supported the French Pope, while most Italian states, England, Portugal, Poland, Hungary and Bohemia backed Urban VI. This confusion lasted for 32 years, from 1377 to 1409. But the worse was still to come.

The Cardinals, concerned about the harm being caused the institutional Church, decided to try to put an end to the conflict. They gathered for a special conclave in the city of Pisa in 1409 where they elected a third man, Pope Alexander V, to be the true Pope. He attempted to depose the other two, but they refused to be deposed. For the next 20 years there were three Popes: one in Rome, one in Avignon, and one in Pisa.

Pope Alexander was succeeded by Pope John XXIII who is considered an Antipope by Catholic historians. In recent years, Cardinal Roncalli, elected as Pope in 1958, chose to be called John XXIV. One day later, however, upon realizing that such a decision would validate the election of John XXIII in 1409, the Vatican announced that Pope Roncalli's name was John XXIII.

For over fifty years (more than a generation of Catholics) the Church of Rome had no definite and clear guide! For more than fifty years, Catholics did not know which of the three was their infallible teacher: the Pope in Rome, the Pope in Avignon, or the Pope in Pisa. This period of Church history is a very significant argument against the Roman Catholic teaching that Christ willed the papacy in order that His Church might have a visible head who will insure that every person knows what he must believe and do in order to be saved.

Papal Definitions Contradict Papal Infallibility!

If Popes are infallible, then they cannot be heretics. A heretical Pope would be an oxymoron. The truth is, however, that there have been Popes in the history of the Church who have been condemned as heretics by Church Councils and even excommunicated by succeeding Popes. These Popes defined as truths what the Roman Catholic Church now condemns as heresies. Their definitions are not about theological trifles, but basic Catholic (and biblical) truths that the Church says must be believed in order for a Roman Catholic to be saved!

Catholics are often defensive when it comes to papal infallibility. When Evangelical Christians question the sinful life and historical or scientific blunders of certain Popes, their answer is always the same: "The dogma of infallibility refers only to matters of faith and morals, and only when the Pope speaks *ex cathedra*, namely as supreme teacher and head of the church." As we will see, these heretical Popes did speak *ex cathedra*. In fact, that is the very reason they were condemned.

Some Popes have been firm, timely and biblical in their definitions. Others have been hesitant and unbiblical. Still others were heretics.

One Pope did not always agree with the next. Take the issue of images, statues, and icons for example. Some Popes permitted it, others disallowed it, depending primarily on the attitude of the Emperor whose favor they may have cherished more than the truth.

Pope Liberius Denied The Deity Of Christ

One of the first major heresies to threaten the Church was Arianism. By denying the deity of Christ, Arius was definitely aiming at the destruction of the true Gospel of salvation. Who opposed Arius with authority and determination? It was Athanasius, bishop of Alexandria. What about Pope Liberius? He sided with Arius and excommunicated Athanasius, who did not give up and kept fighting until justice was done and the truth prevailed. Was this not a basic error in matters of faith? The Catholic Church today tries to minimize the fact by saying that the Pope exercised poor judgment! The truth is better expressed by a canonized Catholic saint and doctor of the Church, Hilary of Poitiers, also called the Athanasius of the West.[1] In his polemic addressed to Pope Liberius he wrote: "I say anathema to thee, Liberius, and to thy accomplices!" Obviously it was a heretical stand the Pope had taken, not merely a poor judgment!

Pope Zosimus First Denied The Necessity Of God's Grace For Salvation And Then Recanted His Position

Something even more embarrassing to the infallible head of the Church of Rome happened about a century later. In North Africa Pelagius and Celestius were practically denying the necessity of God's grace for salvation! This time it was bishop Augustine who championed the battle against such heresy. Where was Pope Zosimus? He was in Rome, acting decisively and authoritatively, but in the wrong direction. He upheld the heretics against Augustine and other orthodox African bishops! There is no doubt that he spoke with the authority of the head of the Church, for he used the words *Apostolicae Sedis Auctoritate* (by the authority of the Apostolic See). He pronounced Pelagius and Celestius as *absolutae fidei* (impeccably in keeping with the faith). Neither did he do it lightly or in a hurry, for, in his words, he had not reached such conclusion "in a hasty or untimely manner." It is interesting to notice that later Pope Zosimus recanted his decision because the Church was following Augustine anyway!

---

[1] Hilary of Poitiers was declared a doctor of the Church by Pope Pius IX in 1851.

Pope Vigilius Was Condemned As A Heretic By The Fifth General Council, Constantinople, AD 553

The Council of Chalcedon (451) rightly excommunicated the Nestorians and Monophysites for heresies concerning the nature of Christ. The Monophysites taught that Jesus had only one nature. The Nestorians taught that He had two personalities. The Word of God teaches that Jesus was God in the flesh, one person with two natures (divine and human). Pope Vigilius first sided with the Monophysites in a work titled "Judicatum." Later, in a second work titled "Constitutum," he embraced the Nestorian view. In this document, Pope Vigilius used the authoritative expression "We ordain and decree . . . ." The Fifth General Council, which met at Constantinople in AD 553 condemned Vigilius as a heretic. Vigilius later recanted and embraced the orthodox teaching of the Council of Chalcedon.

Pope Honorius Was Excommunicated By The Sixth General Council

Pope Honorius embraced the heresy of the Monothelites who taught that Christ had only one will. He was excommunicated by the Sixth General Council. His condemnation was later confirmed by Pope Leo II.

The fact that Councils excommunicated Popes as heretics clearly demonstrates that Popes are not infallible in matters of faith and morals. There can be no question that at this time in history the Church held the authority of the Councils above that of the Popes! Now, however, the dogma of papal infallibility anathematizes such a belief.

Pope Clement VIII Found 3000 Errors
In Pope Sixtus VI's "Infallible" Latin Translation

All took place in the 16th century, when the Pope's authority was much greater. Pope Sixtus V (1585-1590), who was Pope but no scholar, decided to have a second official Latin translation Bible for the Church. Apparently, he thought that his infallible authority would cause him to produce an infallible version! In the introduction to this official version of the Bible he wrote: "By the fullness of the Apostolic power We decree and declare that this edition, approved by the authority delivered to us by the Lord, is to be received and held as true, lawful, authentic and unquestioned in all public and private discussion, reading, preaching and explanations ..." The Pope threatened to anathematize anyone who would make changes in any detail.

Catholic scholars quickly realized that the Pope's edition was the work of a novice, and called for a new edition! Several scholars worked at it. More than 3000 mistakes were found! Pope Clement the VIII faced quite a dilemma as he wrote the preface to the new edition. Considering the solemn and powerful condemnation his successor had sounded against anyone who dared to meddle with his edition, how could he explain the 3000 mistakes without damaging the Papal authority? Following the suggestion of Cardinal Bellarmine, Pope Clement decided to blame all the mistakes on the printers! Instead of obeying the Lord's command, "You shall not bear false witness," he adopted the philosophy of Machiavelli, "The end justifies the means." It was more important to preserve the authority of the Pope than it was to tell the truth!

If Not The Pope, Then Who Is The Church's Infallible Teacher?

Jesus left His Church a clear and unchangeable guide, the written Word of God. God's Word, not the Pope, is the final authority in matters of faith and practice. The apostle Paul testified concerning this when he said:

> [16]*All Scripture is God-breathed and is useful for teaching, rebuking, correcting and training in righteousness,* [17]*so that the man of God may be thoroughly equipped for every good work (2 Timothy 3:16, 17).*

The two verbs "teaching" and "rebuking" in the Greek language have to do with what is true or false. The Bible teaches what is true and exposes what is false. The verbs "correcting and training" have to do with what is right or wrong. The Word of God leads us in the paths of righteousness and convicts us when we wander from that path. God's Word is the final, sure, and sufficient guide for both doctrine and practice.

Jesus also gave his Church an infallible teacher—not the Pope, but the Holy Spirit Himself. Just before going back to the Father after His resurrection, Jesus promised His disciples that He would not leave them as orphans, but that He would send them a Counselor who would be with them forever, and would guide them into all truth.

> [15]*If you love me, you will obey what I command.* [16]*And I will ask the Father, and he will give you another Counselor, to be with you forever—*[17]*the Spirit of truth. The world cannot accept Him, because it neither sees Him nor knows Him. But you know Him, for He lives with you and will be in you.* [18]*I will not leave you as orphans; I will come to you (John 14:15-18).*
>
> *But when he, the Spirit of truth comes, he will guide you into all truth . . . (John 16:13).*

The Holy Spirit guided the Church into all truth by guiding the authors of Scriptures in recording what had been revealed to them and what they had seen. What they wrote under the inspiration of the Holy Spirit was exactly what God intended them to say (2 Timothy 3:16; 2 Peter 1:21). He continues to guide into truth by helping believers to understand and apply the Word of God in their daily lives (1 Corinthians 2:10-14).

One day while talking to a Catholic priest and theology professor, I asked him why the Church needs an "infallible Pope as head of the Church." He answered, *"So that the true Church of Jesus Christ might have a sure and safe guide regarding the truth!"* I objected, *"It took the Pope more than eleven centuries to decide that priests, bishops and Popes had to be celibate. It took him over eighteen centuries to decide that the Pope is infallible, and that Mary, the mother of Jesus, was conceived without sin and lived a sinless life. It took him more than nineteen centuries to decide that Mary had been taken up to heaven body and soul. If he had the infallible assistance of the Holy Spirit, why did it take him so long? Why did he leave the Church in error and doubt for so long?"* The theologian-priest was confused. He tried to answer, but could not. The truth is that Catholics have no answer to all this.

The only sure and safe guide in matters of faith and practice is the message of the apostles and prophets, accurately recorded under the inspiration of the Holy Spirit in the Holy Scriptures. This true and unchanging Word of God stands forever!

Conclusion

I realize that I have written things that may be unpleasant or even offensive to some. However, I believe Catholics need to know these things so they can make free and intelligent choices concerning their faith. To hide them or cover them up would be deception!

Immediately after saying *"You are Peter, and upon this rock I will build my church,"* Jesus rebuked Peter saying, *"Get behind me, Satan!"* Jesus did not hide Peter's errors. He would not hide the errors of Peter's "successors" either!

Review The Following:

♦ Where were the three seats of power in the Roman Catholic Church between 1409 and 1429 (see p. 206)?

♦ What was the name of the Italian Pope elected in 1309 (see p. 205)?

♦ What was the name of the French Pope elected while Pope Urban VI still lived (see p. 206)?

♦ What was the name of the Pope elected by the conclave at Pisa in 1409 who attempted to depose the other two Popes in Avignon and Rome (see p. 206)?

♦ What major orthodox doctrine did Pope Liberius deny (see p. 208)?

♦ With whom did Pope Liberius side (see p. 208)?

♦ What did Pope Liberius do to Athanasius for opposing Arianism (see p. 208)?

♦ Who were the two heretics with which Pope Zosimus initially sided (see p. 208)?

♦ What evidence is there to indicate that Pope Zosimus did speak *ex cathedra* in siding with these heretics (see p. 208)?

♦ Who opposed these two heretics (see p. 208)?

♦ What caused Pope Zosimus to change his mind (see p. 208)?

♦ Which Council condemned Pope Vigilius (see p. 209)?

♦ Why did they condemn him (see p. 209)?

♦ How did Pope Vigilius respond to their actions (see p. 209)?

♦ Which Council excommunicated Pope Honorius (see p. 209)?

♦ How does the excommunication of a Pope by a council call into question the dogma of the infallibility of the Pope (see p. 209)?

◆ Which Pope presided over the first translation of the Latin Vulgate (see p. 210)?

◆ What did he write in the introduction to his translation concerning anyone who would change it (see p. 210)?

◆ How many mistakes did Catholic scholars find in this authoritative version (p. 210)?

◆ How did Pope Clement VIII explain the errors in his predecessor's version (see p. 210)?

◆ Whom did Jesus say He would send to guide us into all truth (see p. 211)?

◆ How does the Holy Spirit guide the Church into all truth (see p. 212)?

◆ What written document should be the final authority in matters of faith and practice (see p. 212)?

◆ If forced to choose between the teachings of a particular church, a Pope, or a pastor, and the teachings of the Word of God, which should we choose to believe and follow?

♦ Why is it important for a believer to study the Word of God?

____ Because as we study His Word, the Holy Spirit guides us into truth

____ Because God's Word is the final authority in matters of faith and practice

____ Because God's Word is a lamp to my feet and a light to my path

____ All of the above

____ None of the above

♦ Set a goal for yourself in terms of Bible study for this next year. Check one or more of the following.

____ I will make it my goal to read the Bible for at least five minutes every day.

____ I will make it my goal to read through the entire Bible once this year.

____ I will make it my goal to read at least one chapter in the Bible every day.

____ I will make it my goal to memorize 50 verses from the Bible this year.

____ I will make it my goal to attend a church where the Word of God is preached every Sunday this year.

____ Other:_____

Chapter 15

The Truth About Idolatry

I was a director of a Catholic seminary when a Pentecostal pastor visited me in my office, offering New Testaments for the boys at the Youth Center. I invited him to see our new church building, of which I was quite proud. As we toured the cathedral, he commented that he did not think it was right to make images and set them up in the church.

As a priest I had my answer ready: "Even God ordered Moses to make a bronze serpent!"

Quietly he answered, "Look up 2 Kings 18 and see what happened to the serpent Moses built."

As he left, moved more by curiosity than a desire to know the truth, I opened to 2 Kings 18 and read that Hezekiah *"did what was right in the eyes of the Lord . . . . He broke into pieces the bronze snake Moses had made, for up to that time the Israelites had been burning incense to it"* (2 Kings 18:3-5).

A few days later, while celebrating a solemn mass in honor of Mary Immaculate, I offered incense to a statue of her. I was startled by the remembrance of what the pastor had told me and what I read in the Book of Kings. I sensed there was something wong in what I was doing.

God Alone Is To Be Worshiped

Worship is the natural response of the heart of one who knows and walks with the living, true God. He marvels at the wisdom of God. He is awestruck by His majesty and power, and wonders at His love. God is his first desire, his first love, the focus of his thoughts and affections.

There is a very special place in the believer's heart for God, even as there is a place reserved in the heart of a faithful wife for her husband. The comparison is not at all presumptuous. The Church is called "the bride of Christ," and as such owes Him its loyalty. Ezekiel likens idolatry to prostitution and adultery (Ezekiel 16:15-22).

God, our Creator, is jealous for our worship. Worship is simply the expression of great reverence, respect, and admiration. When properly directed, it is declaring God's worthiness, or ascribing to Him the glory due His name (Psalm 29:2). The sin of idolatry is that of attributing to some created, or even man-made, thing what is properly due to God. That is why God protests the idolatry in Judah by saying "I will not give my glory to another, or my praise to idols."

Following this principle, God, ALONE, is the Creator; no other should be praised as such. God is the ONLY one who is able to satisfy our deepest needs; He should be honored as such. God is our refuge and strength; He should be trusted as such.

Idolatry, then, is more than just calling a man-made image "God," and worshiping a stone or a stick. Very few in the modern world would entertain such an absurdity. (I doubt that men in the ancient world believed that way either. I suspect their images merely represented their gods). Idolatry is directing honor, praise, respect, or affection that rightly belongs to God to some created person or thing. Thus, greed is idolatry because the greedy man has focused his affections on THINGS rather than God (Colossians 3:5). In the same way, praying to other than God is idolatry, inasmuch as the one asking fixes his hope on someone other than God to help or to save, and ascribes to someone other than God the attributes of omnipresence (ability to hear the request), omniscience (ability to know what is best), and even omnipotence (ability to give what is being sought).

God Forbids The Use Of Images

In 1989 I had the privilege of speaking at the University of the Philippines' "Christ's Awareness Week" organized by Campus Crusade for Christ and Intervarsity Christian Fellowship. One of the highlights of the program was a panel discussion where two Roman Catholic priests and myself would share some twenty minutes each and then answer questions during an open forum. The auditorium was packed. I was told that almost 80% of the 300 who participated were Roman Catholics.

I was given double time because one of the priests arrived late. I was truly astonished at how coldly these Catholic students received the Catholic priest's message. When my turn came, every single time I quoted God's Word, there was an ovation! My surprise reached its climax during the open forum.

A Catholic student asked why the Catholic Church erased the second commandment from the decalogue given by Moses: "You shall not make for yourself idols ... and you shall not bow down to them" (Exodus 20:4). The Catholic priest, who had a doctorate in Holy Scriptures earned in Rome, responded by saying that this commandment was only for the Israelites, who started worshiping idols in the desert. He continued by saying that it was a big mistake to believe that this commandment should apply to the 20th century. *"Holy*

Scriptures," he insisted, *"should never be taken out of context, as Evangelicals do when they apply this commandment to Christians in our time!"*

It was my time to respond. After silent prayer in my heart, I simply asked the priest to explain what was the time and context of this commandment. After he repeated that it was during the Israelites' exodus from Egypt, I asked: *"And what is the time and context of the other nine commandments?"* After several embarrassing seconds of silence, he honestly said: *"Well, the time was the same, and the context . . . the same, too."* Of course he couldn't answer otherwise, because people in the auditorium well knew that God had given all of the ten commandments at the same time and in the same circumstances. So I insisted: *"Does the Roman Catholic Church accept the sixth and seventh commandments* (for Catholics, the fifth and sixth): *You shall not kill. You shall not commit adultery'?"* His answer, obviously, had to be yes! *"To be consistent,"* I concluded, *"the Roman Catholic Church should also reject these two commandments, because they were given at the same time and in the same historical context as the second!"* There was a standing ovation after this statement. I almost felt bad for the Catholic priest! I wish he could have given a better answer.

Roman Catholic theologians sometimes argue that the command not to make an idol or bow down

Roman Catholics are truly misled whenever they are taught that the second commandment does not apply to our time or is a simple repetition of the first.

to it is a repetition of the first commandment, "You shall have no other gods before me." Although the two commands are related to each other, they are substantially different. The first command *(You shall have no other gods before me)*, tells **who** we are to worship. The second, *(You shall not make an idol)* tells **how** we are to worship. It is possible to worship the right God in the wrong way.

♦ Read the second commandment, quoted below from the Holy Scriptures, and then answer the following questions.

> *⁴You shall not make for yourself an idol in the form of anything in heaven above or on the earth, beneath or in the waters below. ⁵You shall not bow down to them or worship them; for I, the LORD your God, am a jealous God, punishing the children for the sin of the fathers to the third and fourth generation of those who hate me, ⁶but showing love to a thousand generations of those who love me and keep my commandments (Exodus 20:4-6).*

1. What is the context of these verses?

2. What does this second commandment forbid (verses 4 and 5)?

3. What does God promise those who do make, worship, or bow down to images (verse 5)?

4. Which of the following statements is true according to the second commandment?

   _____ Bowing down before an image is an act of hatred to God that will be punished.

   _____ Bowing down before an image is an act of love for God that will be rewarded.

Catholic Images Are Worshiped!

Some seek to justify the use of images by saying they do not worship their images, but merely honor or venerate the saints whom these images represent. What is the difference between worshiping an idol and honoring a saint?

"Worship" can be distinguished from "honor" by both internal and external factors. Internally, worship is evidenced by fear. If a person is afraid to remove an image from his home or business for fear something bad might happen, if he puts an image in his home or business believing that its presence will bring blessing, or if he believes that the presence of an image insures safety in travel or protection from harm, he is worshiping the image. Externally, worship is expressed by actions such as bowing before the image, kneeling before it, crawling up to it, kissing it, affectionately touching it, praying to it, dressing it in fine clothes, burning candles before it and offering it gifts.

♦   Read the following verses and answer the questions below.

> ²This is what the LORD says: "Do not learn the ways of the nations . . . . ³For the customs of the people are worthless; they cut a tree out of the forest and a craftsman shapes it with his chisel. ⁴They adorn it with silver and gold . . . . ⁹What the craftsman and goldsmith have made is then dressed in blue and purple—all made by skilled workers" (Jeremiah 10:2, 4, 9).

♦   What does God forbid in these verses?

♦ What are the similarities in these verses between the way the heathen dressed their images and the way Catholics treat their Santo Niños today?

> *⁹All who make idols are nothing, and the things they treasure are worthless . . . ¹³The carpenter measures with a line and makes an outline with a marker; he roughs it out with chisels and marks it with compasses. He shapes it in the form of man, of man in all his glory, that it may dwell in a shrine (Isaiah 44:9, 13).*

♦ Where did the heathen put their idols according to the verse quoted above?

♦ How is this similar to the way Catholic images are treated?

> *⁵To whom will you compare me or count me equal? To whom will you liken me that we may be compared? ⁶Some pour out gold from their bags and weigh out silver on the scales; they hire a goldsmith to make it into a god, and they bow down and worship it. ⁷They lift it to their shoulders and carry it; they set it up in its place, and there it stands. From that spot it cannot move. Though one cries out to it, it does not answer; it cannot save him from his troubles (Isaiah 46:5-7).*

♦ What did the heathen do with their images that the goldsmith made, according to verse 6 above?

♦ What did the heathen do with their images according to verse 7 above?

♦ How does this compare with what is done with Catholic images during fiestas, Holy Week, and other such occasions?

> [16]*Half the wood he burns in the fire; over it he prepares his meal, he roasts his meat and eats his fill. He also warms himself and says, "Ah! I am warm; I see the fire."* [17]*From the rest he makes a god, his idol; he bows down to it and worships. He prays to it and says, "Save me; you are my god" (Isaiah 44:16-17).*

♦ According to the verses quoted above, what did the heathen do before their images?

♦ Are there similarities between what they did and what Catholics do before the images of Mary?

> In 1 Kings 19:18 God speaks to Elijah and says: *"Yet I reserve seven thousand in Israel—all whose knees have not bowed down to Baal and all whose mouths have not kissed him."*

♦ In addition to bowing their knees before Baal, what did the heathen do with their mouths according to the verse quoted above?

♦ How is this similar to what Catholics are doing with their images?

REASONS WHY GOD FORBIDS THE MAKING OF IMAGES

1. God Is A Jealous God.

> *23Be careful not to forget the covenant of the LORD your God that he made with you; do not make for yourselves an idol in the form of anything the LORD your God has forbidden. 24For the LORD your God is a consuming fire, a jealous God (Deuteronomy 4:23, 24).*

Holy Scriptures teach us that God is jealous for the worship and adoration of His people. In the Old Testament God loved His people Israel with a special love, compared to that of a husband for his wife (Isaiah 54:5; Jeremiah 3:14, 20). In the New Testament, Christ's love for the Church is compared to the love of a husband for his wife (Ephesians 5:25). The Church is called the Bride of Christ (Revelation 19:7; 21:2, 9; 22:17). This explains God's jealousy: when a person worships or bows down to an image, he or she is committing spiritual adultery.

> *... you made yourself male idols and engaged in prostitution with them. And you took your embroidered clothes to put on them, and you offered my oil and incense before them (Ezekiel 16:17).*

God forbids the making of images. He knows that an image made to represent a powerful being or person other than God will cause people to commit spiritual adultery, drawing their affections away from God and fixing them on another.

2.   No Image Can Truly Represent God.

To whom, then, will you compare God? What image will you compare him to? (Isaiah 40:18)

God is spirit. He has no physical likeness. No image can accurately depict Him. Any image made to represent Him would be demeaning to Him.

The Worship Of Images Is A Grievous Sin

I have met many Catholic and even some Protestant leaders who maintain that Evangelicals are too fussy about the Catholic form of worship! They think that the word "idols" does not refer to the images and icons, or statues of Christ, Mary and the saints, used by the Catholic and Greek Orthodox Church as well as by many Charismatic groups. They add that the idols of Scripture are the objects of pagan worship only, such as the sun, the moon, the stars, various animals and the gods of the pagans. Moreover, they want us to believe that if people also worship the true God, the use of images, statues, and icons cannot be considered idolatry.

It is difficult for me to understand how people can so easily ignore the gravity and terrible consequences of idolatry, or simply excuse it by calling it *veneration* or *honor* instead of worship. The Biblical teaching on the subject is plain. Paul writes forthrightly of God's wrath against the godlessness and wickedness of men who *"exchanged the glory of the immortal God for images made to look like mortal man"* (Romans 1:23).

The Greek word translated *mortal man* means *human being,* referring to images of both man and woman![1] God said

---

[1] ανθρωπου, not ανηρ.

the same thing to Moses:

> *¹⁵You saw no form of any kind the day the LORD spoke to you at Horeb out of the fire. Therefore watch yourselves very carefully, ¹⁶so that you do not become corrupt and make for yourselves an idol, an image of any shape, whether formed like a man or a woman, ¹⁷or like any animal on earth . . . ¹⁹And when you look up to the sky and see the sun, the moon, and the stars—all the heavenly array—do not be enticed into bowing down to them and worshiping things the LORD your God has apportioned to all the nations under heaven (Deuteronomy 4:15-19).*

God not only classifies images made like animals or objects of nature as idols, but also images made in the form of a man or a woman. This includes images of Mary, the saints, angels, and even the images of Jesus. No person of the Trinity (Father, Son, or Holy Spirit) must ever be represented by any image. As Jesus taught the woman at the well: *God is spirit, and His worshipers must worship in spirit and in truth* (John 4:24).

Idolatry Leads To Other Sins

> *²²Although they claimed to be wise, they became fools ²³and exchanged the glory of the immortal God for images made to look like mortal man and birds and animals and reptiles. ²⁴Therefore God gave them over in the sinful desires of their hearts to sexual impurity for the degrading of their bodies with one another. ²⁵They exchanged the truth of God for a lie, and worshiped and served created things rather than the Creator—who is forever praised. Amen. ²⁶Because of this, God gave them over to shameful lusts. Even their women exchanged natural relations for unnatural ones. ²⁷In the same way men also abandoned natural relations with women and were*

inflamed with lust for one another. Men committed indecent acts with other men, and received in themselves the due penalty for their perversion (Romans 1:22-27). [Emphasis mine]

I gauge the gravity of the sin of idolatry from its consequences, as described by the apostle Paul. The two

God gave mankind up to the sinful desires of their hearts because of idolatry.

introductory Greek conjunctions translated as *therefore* in verse 24 and *because of this* in verse 26, clearly teach that the worst sins of immorality mentioned in these verses (promiscuity, adultery, homosexuality in general and lesbianism in particular) are a *result* of idolatry!

How is it then that Roman Catholics, while rightly and strongly condemning all the sins of immorality mentioned above, *accept and encourage* idolatry, which is clearly condemned in Scripture and singled out by God Himself as being the cause of other sins?

Idolatry Is The Worship Of Demons

[19]Do I mean then that a sacrifice offered to an idol is anything, or that an idol is anything? [20]No, but the sacrifices of pagans are offered to demons, not to God, and I do not want you to be participants with demons (1 Corinthians 10:19, 20).

♦ Who are idol worshipers actually worshiping according to these verses?

♦ How might this explain the seemingly miraculous powers attached to certain images?

God Wants Imageless Worship

In the fourth chapter of John's Gospel we read an episode in the life of Jesus when he met a Samaritan woman at Jacob's well. Part of the background to this story is an ongoing controversy between the Jews and Samaritans on the subject of worship. The Jews argued that people must worship God at the temple in Jerusalem. The Samaritan Scriptures taught that Mount Gerizim (rather than Mount Ebal) was the place God had commanded an altar to be built (Deuteronomy 27:4-6). In 400 BC, the Samaritans built a temple on Mount Gerizim. In 128 BC, the Jews destroyed it.

Jesus started out with the woman at the well by revealing some details of her sinful life. This made her uncomfortable, and she decided to change the subject. She said: *I can see that you are a prophet. Our fathers worshiped on this mountain, but you Jews claim that the place where we must worship is in Jerusalem.* Jesus went along with the change of topic, and clearly stated to the Samaritan woman that salvation came from the Jews.

> *You Samaritans worship what you do not know; we worship what we do know, for salvation is from the Jews (John 4:22).*

Although the woman's question regarded the *place* of worship, Jesus answered by addressing its *substance*. Samaritans followed many pagan idolatrous practices in their worship! The real issue, then, that needed to be addressed was not *where* they worshiped, but *how*. Thus, Jesus continued:

> [23]*Yet a time is coming and has now come when the true worshipers will worship the Father in spirit and truth, for they are the kind of worshipers the Father seeks.* [24]*God is spirit, and his worshipers must worship in spirit and in truth (John 4:23-24).*

This passage, speaking of true worshipers, implies that there are false ones. All those who make use of idols, and do not worship in spirit and in truth, are false worshipers.

♦ Read the following verses and answer the questions below.

> ²⁵*The images of their gods you are to burn in the fire. Do not covet the silver and gold on them, and do not take it for yourselves, or you will be ensnared by it, for it is detestable to the* LORD *your God.* ²⁶*Do not bring a detestable thing into your house or you, like it, will be set apart for destruction. Utterly abhor and detest it, for it is set apart for destruction (Deuteronomy 7:25-26).*

♦ According to the verses quoted above, what does the LORD want us to do with our images?

♦ If the images in our home belong to our parents or our unbelieving husband or wife, what should we do? Why?

♦ Why does God command us to destroy the images in fire, and not even to covet the gold in them? Why can't we give them to our neighbor or hide them in a closet upstairs?

Conclusion

♦ Why is idolatry like adultery (see p. 218)?

♦ What is worship (see p. 218)?
   Worship is the expression of great _____, respect, and admiration.
   Worship is declaring God's worthiness, or ascribing to Him the ____ due His name.

♦ What is idolatry (see p. 218)?
   It is _____ to some created thing what is properly due to God.

♦ Why is greed a form of idolatry (Colossians 3:5) (see p. 219)?

♦ To what does Ezekiel compare idolatry in Ezekiel 16:17 (see p. 225)?

♦ What does Ezekiel 16:17 teach us about how God feels when those who claim to be "His" continue to worship images (see pp. 225-226)?

Appendix I

The Development of Catholic Doctrines

Most Roman Catholics, especially those who never question the teachings of their Church, assume that all basic doctrines and practices date back to the teachings of Jesus and the time of the apostles. For the sake of truth, here are the dates (sometimes approximate, sometimes exact), of many unbiblical Roman Catholic doctrines, practices, and laws.

1. Elders or Presbyters first
   called Priests by Lucian — End of 2nd century
2. Sacerdotal mass started by
   Cyprian — End of 3rd century
3. Prayers for the dead — About AD 300
4. Making the sign of the cross — About AD 300
5. Wax candles — About AD 320
6. Veneration of angels and saints,
   and use of images — AD 375
7. The mass celebrated daily,
   instead of Sundays only — AD 394

8. Exaltation of Mary as "Mother of God" (Council of Ephesus) — AD 431

9. Priests wearing special vestments — About AD 500

10. Extreme Unction (anointing of the sick) as a sacrament — AD 526

11. The doctrine of Purgatory (by Gregory I) — AD 593

12. Latin to be used in worship — AD 600

13. Prayers addressed to Mary, angels and dead saints — AD 600

14. First time for the bishop of Rome to be called "Pope" (Boniface I) — AD 610

15. Kissing the Pope's feet — AD 709

16. The Pope declared a State Sovereign by Pepin, King of the Franks — AD 750

17. Veneration of crosses, relics and images of the saints — AD 786

18. Water, blessed by a priest with a pinch of salt, becomes "holy water" — AD 850

19. Special veneration of St. Joseph, the foster-father of Jesus — AD 890

20. Beginning of the College of Cardinals (electors of the Pope) — AD 927

21. Church bells first baptized by Pope John XIII (Baptism of bells) — AD 965

22. Canonization of dead saints for the first time by Pope John XV — AD 995

23. Fast and abstinence from meat on Fridays of Lent — AD 998

24. Mass as a sacrifice and grave obligation of Sunday attendance — 11th century

25. Obligatory celibacy for priests and bishops — AD 1079

26. The Rosary introduced (adopted from pagans?) by Peter the Hermit — AD 1090

27. Inquisition instituted by the
    Council of Verona   AD 1184
28. Sale of Indulgences   AD 1190
29. Doctrine of Seven Sacraments
    introduced by Peter Lombard   12th century
30. Transubstantiation defined by
    Pope Innocent III   AD 1215
31. Adoration of the Host (worship
    of wafer) decreed by
    Pope Honorius III   AD 1220
32. Bible on "Index of Forbidden
    Books" for laymen (Council
    of Valencia)   AD 1229
33. Use of scapular devised by
    Simon Stock of England   AD 1251
34. The cup (consecrated wine)
    forbidden to the laity (Council
    of Constance)   AD 1414
35. Secret confession of sins to a
    priest instead of God (Innocent III)   AD 1215
36. Purgatory defined a dogma at
    Council of Florence   AD 1439
37. Tradition of equal authority with
    the Bible (Council of Trent)   AD 1545
38. Apocryphal books declared
    canonical and added to the Bible   AD 1546
39. New Longer Creed in place of
    Apostolic Creed by Pope Pius IV   AD 1560
40. Immaculate Conception of Mary
    defined a major dogma by
    Pope Pius IX   AD 1854

41. Syllabus of Errors* proclaimed
    by Pius IX   AD 1864
42. Infallibility of the Pope defined
    a major dogma by Pius IX   AD 1870
43. Assumption of Mary body and soul
    defined a major dogma by Pius XII   AD 1950
44. Mary proclaimed Mother of the
    Church by Paul VI   AD 1965

*The "Syllabus of Errors" contained official condemnation of Freedom of Religion, Freedom of Conscience and Freedom of Speech. It also disapproved of Freedom of the Press, and condemned all Scientific Discoveries not in keeping with Roman Catholic teachings. It once more asserted the Pope's temporal authority over all civil rulers.

Appendix II

Purgatory and Vicarious Suffering

We have already proved how the doctrine of purgatory, apparently considered a not-so-important teaching by Catholics and many Protestants, is a practical denial of salvation by faith and of the sufficiency of Christ's sacrifice. Far from being a minor doctrine, it has an extremely important part in the life of Catholics.

The doctrine was officially introduced by Pope Gregory I in AD 593, but it was defined a dogma only during the Council of Florence in AD 1439, and solemnly confirmed over a century later at the Council of Trent. This doctrine is the reason why many Catholics, especially rich ones, spend a lot of money to have masses celebrated for their departed loved ones. They believe that almost all adult Catholics who do not go to hell will have to spend some time in purgatory before being admitted to heaven. The masses allegedly get people out of purgatory and into heaven.

Only baptized infants and little children go straight to heaven after death! Extremely few adults make it straight to heaven—only those privileged "saints" who die without any unconfessed big or small sin after doing complete penance of any sin they may have committed. One can never be sure that his penance is complete! Therefore, living relatives spend sacrificially to offer as many masses and prayers as possible so that their time of suffering in purgatory may be shortened.

Many Roman Catholics, particularly nuns and monks, offer their lives and sufferings for the salvation of others! During my high school and college days in the seminary, I was frequently encouraged to choose voluntary sufferings and hardships and offer them to God as payment for the sins of some bad relative either still living or dead. Such practices are quite common in the Church of Rome, and many canonized saints are praised for suffering in this way! The famous Padre Pio, considered a living saint because of his bleeding hands during mass, once wrote to his Provincial Superior:

> *My dear Father, I want to ask you permission to do something. For some time past I have felt the need to offer myself to the Lord as a victim for poor sinners and for the souls in Purgatory. I have begged the Lord to pour out upon me the punishment prepared for these souls, so that they may be consoled and quickly admitted to Paradise (Newsletter: The Padre Pio Foundation of America and the Mass Association, August 1988, p. 2).*

I had similar noble desires when I was young. But these desires reflect a total ignorance of the true Gospel. Such belief and practice is nothing short of an insult to the all-sufficient vicarious sacrifice of Jesus, and an outright denial of the Gospel of Grace. It also attaches a very presumptuous attitude—thinking ourselves better than others and imagining that God will accept our sacrifices as payment for other people's sins. The truth is we cannot even pay for our own!

Padre Pio was famous the world over. Innumerable thousands of tourists and pilgrims visited him, trying to assist at his mass! He claimed one time that millions of souls of the dead had attended his masses, and had "stopped in his cell to thank him for his help on their way [from purgatory] to Paradise!" He claims to have literally seen them with "physical eyes!" Obviously he was deluded by Satan and filled with spiritual pride.[1]

---

[1]Ibid, p. 3.

Appendix III

The Scapular

One of the ways for a Catholic to shorten his days in purgatory, or to make sure that he will not go to hell, is to wear the scapular. The scapular consists of two tiny pieces of cloth, generally brown, mostly worn by women. On one side it contains an image of the child Jesus, on the other Mary's promise that any one who dies wearing it will never go to hell! Mary allegedly made this great promise to Simon Stock on July 16, 1251.

Almost a century later, another promise or privilege was added by Pope John XXII (1322): "I, the Mother of Grace, shall descend on the Saturday after their death, and whosoever I shall find in Purgatory [wearing the scapular at the hour of death], I shall free [for heaven]!" This is officially called the Sabbatine Privilege.

In the conclusion of Simon Stock's prayer, he says: "O sweet Heart of Mary, be our salvation!" This is the saddest part of it all: Mary has taken the place of our Savior in the hearts of so many people!

Appendix IV

Baptismal Regeneration

*B*aptism for Roman Catholics is, as we saw in the chapter on salvation, the means through which a person is born again. It is, therefore, necessary for salvation. Catechism defines baptism as "the true sacrament of the dead," for only unregenerate people, who are spiritually dead, may receive it. Confession, also called the Sacrament of Penance, becomes a sacrament of the dead only when a Catholic has committed a mortal (deadly) sin, which causes one to spiritually die again.

Studying God's Word regarding baptism, Evangelicals generally come to the opposite conclusion. Baptism is a command of Christ **for those who believe**, for those who are spiritually alive through faith! Because it is a command, it is a duty for all true believers to obey it. But, like other commands, it cannot be considered necessary for salvation, either alone or added to faith!

The passage most often quoted by Catholics, Orthodox, and even some Protestants in support of infant baptism is found in the sixteenth chapter of the Book of Acts. Here a certain jailer in Philippi asks the apostle Paul, "What must I do to be saved?" Paul answers: *"Believe in the Lord Jesus, and you will be saved—you and your household . . . Then immediately he and all his family were baptized"* (Acts 16:31, 33). Those who argue for infant baptism justify their practice by the expression "and all his household." They assume that there were small children in the household.

I would like to point out, first of all, that Paul connected salvation with faith. Baptism followed. Furthermore, verse 32 says:

> *Then they spoke the word of the Lord to him and to all the others in the house (Acts 16:32). [Emphasis mine]*

This took place before they were baptized! So baptism was logically administered to "all" those who had heard, understood and believed the Word! This is verified for us in verse 34:

> *. . . the whole family was filled with joy, because they had come to believe in God (Acts 16:34).*

The expression "all his family was baptized" (verse 33) must include the same people as in the preceding verse, "they spoke the word to all the others in the house" (verse 32), and the one that follows, "the whole family was filled with joy, because they had come to believe" (verse 34).

Two other simple observations: (1) People take for granted that there were infants and little children in the family! It is true that most families have them, but not all! (2) The text and context state specifically that all took place in the heart of the night. At that time, generally, infants and little children are sleeping!

Infants and little children are unable to understand the Word and to believe in God! So we do not baptize them.

Jesus spoke of the absolute necessity of faith hundreds of times! Only twice He mentions baptism together with faith or the preaching of the Gospel. Moreover, if baptism were sufficient for infants and little children and necessary for adults in order to be saved, I would expect Jesus to baptize as many as possible. The truth is that the Gospels do not record even one single instance!

The same can almost be said about the apostle Paul, the greatest New Testament theologian and evangelist. His heart's desire and prayer to God was that his people, the Israelites, should be saved (Cf. Romans 10:1). If baptism were necessary for salvation, I would expect him to baptize as many as possible. On the contrary, he writes to the church of Corinth:

> *[14]I am thankful that I did not baptize any of you except Crispus and Gaius, [15]so that no one can say that you were baptized into my name. [16]Yes, I also baptized the household of Stephanas; beyond that, I do not remember if I baptized anyone else (1 Corinthians 1:14-16).*

Someone else must have baptized the Corinthian believers. Yet Paul considers all of them his spiritual children: ... *For in Christ Jesus I became your father through the Gospel (1 Corinthians 4:15b).* They had all been born again because they had heard Paul's preaching of the Gospel and believed in Christ, even though the apostle had baptized only a few.

Appendix V

Confession to a Priest

*T*he Roman Catholic Church claims to have the power to forgive the sins of baptized Catholics who make a satisfactory confession to a priest. In an effort to defend this practice (referred to as the Sacrament of Penance), Roman Catholic theologians inevitably quote the words of Jesus to the disciples in the upper room:

> *If you forgive anyone his sins, they are forgiven; if you do not forgive them, they are not forgiven (John 20:23).*

The Sacrament of Penance is only for baptized Catholics. No sacrament except baptism (which is administered to the unregenerate) can be lawfully received, except by baptized Catholics.

The passage in John cannot be used to support the Sacrament of Penance for the following reasons:

1. Jesus was talking to his disciples, not to priests and bishops. There is absolutely no biblical record of His consecrating priests! If there remains any doubt in your mind about this, read the chapter on priesthood again.

2. The context of John 20 is not forgiveness of sins of people who believe (baptized Catholics), but of *unbelievers*. As a matter of fact, this passage is considered to be John's great commission, parallel to Matthew 28:19-20. In the preceding verses Jesus had said:

    Peace be with you! As the Father has sent me, I am sending you (John 20:22).

    Jesus is dealing here with the forgiveness of sins of unbelievers, which takes place when the Gospel is preached and people believe, as we explained in the case of Jesus' words to Peter and the disciples in Matthew 18:18.

3. The disciples to whom Jesus spoke did not understand Him to be giving them authority to forgive sins in a confessional.

    If they understood Him to be instituting the Sacrament of Penance, we would expect to see them practicing it in the book of Acts. However, we find no such practice in the early church. Peter and the other apostles did not set up confessional boxes in the synagogues or in homes. They did not teach people to confess to them their sins. They did not make confession of sins—secret or known—a requirement for receiving forgiveness. They simply preached the Word of God and proclaimed forgiveness of sins for all who would repent, believe, and confess their sins to God!

    By his words, "If you forgive anyone his sins, they are forgiven; if you do not forgive them, they are not forgiven," Jesus was not instituting a Sacrament of Penance. Rather he was giving his disciples the right to proclaim the forgiveness of sins.

    In the Greek, the verb tenses here are very important. The verbs "forgive" and "not forgive" are in the aorist tense, and refer to a one-time action by the disciples. The verbs "are forgiven" and "are not forgiven" are in the perfect tense and refer to an action by God that precedes the disciples' action. Therefore, the disciples' action is a proclamation and confirmation of what God has already done.[2]

God forgives those who repent and believe on the Lord Jesus, not those who confess to a priest. His disciples proclaim and confirm this forgiveness by the preaching of the Gospel.

The above interpretation of John 20:23 is confirmed by the activities of the apostles in the early church. While they did not set up confessional boxes, they did proclaim forgiveness of sins through the preaching of the Gospel (Acts 2:38; 5:31; 10:43; 13:38; 26:18).

Regarding the forgiveness of believer's sins, God's Word is simple and clear:

> *If we confess our sins, he is faithful and just and will forgive us our sins and purify us from all unrighteousness (1 John 1:9).*

Of course, Roman Catholic priests quote this verse, but they use it in the context of Catholic teaching, making people think that confessing means going to the confessional box and to the priest. This is deception. At the time the apostle John wrote these inspired words, there were no priests and no confessionals! There is no *Sacrament of Penance* nor confession to a priest in the Bible. For believers who sin, there is only humble and sincere confession to the Lord.

I was always struck by the Bible's words attributed to God when believers confess their sins to Him: *He is faithful and just to forgive.* I would expect the Bible to say: He is loving and merciful! Of course God is loving and merciful, but as I studied and better understood the reality of the Gospel, I realized that the word "faithful" means that God keeps His word! And

---

[2]Even according to Catholic teaching, the priests' absolution is void if the penitent is not repentant!

His word is that when we truly trust Jesus as Lord and Savior, all our sins are forgiven—past, present and future. The word "just" means that God does what has to be done. The sins that believers confess to Him have already been paid for by His own Son, so that God must forgive. It might sound presumptuous to write such an expression, but His Word says that God is *faithful and just and will forgive us our sins and purify us from all unrighteousness (1 John 1:9).*

Confessing sins to one another has nothing to do with the Sacrament of Penance, either (James 5:16). It has to do with our obligation to those we have offended or who have offended us. We must reconcile with them as well as with God. It does not entail in any way confession to a priest.

Appendix VI

Abortion and Birth Control

*E*vangelicals reject abortion. They believe in the sacredness of human life from conception. Abortion is the murder of a defenseless unborn baby! But artificial birth control is a different issue. Most Evangelicals have no problem with it; and, therefore, strongly disagree with the papal encyclical *Humanae Vitae* of Pope Paul VI condemning the use of contraceptives as gravely sinful. In my opinion the Popes and the Roman Catholic theologians make a fourfold mistake in condemning artificial birth control.

1. **Biblical mistakes**. Catholic leaders use a Scripture passage in the Old Testament to prove that God condemns an incomplete sex act, quoting the case of Onan in Genesis 38:9. They fail to realize that in the context God caused Onan to die, not because of the incomplete sexual act, but because he broke the Levirate Law, by which a man had to give offspring to his deceased brother through the sister-in-law (Levir is Latin for brother-in-law). Such a law

is laid down as a legal obligation in Deuteronomy 25:2-5 and is also mentioned, though in a broader sense, in Ruth 4:5 and 3:12.

Roman Catholic leaders also teach that the main purpose of marriage is having children! Although children are a blessing from God and also one of the purposes of marriage, they are not the primary reason why God gave Eve to Adam. The primary purpose of marriage is the mutual, physical, emotional and spiritual fulfillment of man and woman. At creation, when God first gave Eve to Adam, there was no mention of children. Only later the command was given to go and multiply, and mankind has fulfilled this command. There should be no outside interference with a couple's decision as to how many children they should have, but they should be allowed to know the truth and have access to means that insure responsible parenthood.

In the Bible we have a whole book on love between husband and wife. The *Song of Songs* contains expressions of deep love and mutual fulfillment and pleasurable experiences. There is not a single mention of children!

2. **Scientific mistake.** The Catholic clergy keeps teaching that artificial birth control, like abortion, destroys human life. This is scientifically false! Most forms of artificial birth control aim at preventing conception, so that the term *birth control* is almost a misnomer. It should be *conception control!* It is true, as Catholics insist, that the male sperm and female ovum are the essential parts of human conception, but neither is human life in itself. Life begins when they come together. In the same way, hydrogen and oxygen are essential parts of water, but they are not water until they come together.

3. **Emotional mistake.** The Catholic Church allows and encourages only the so-called "natural" birth control. This is still birth control! This method of birth control, however, does not give consideration to the woman, who actually desires and needs sexual union most when she is fertile.

4. **Social mistake.** The problems of over-population, poverty, ignorance and misery, not to mention the related problems of violence, crime and disease, are ever increasing. The sub-human conditions in which millions and millions of children and adults in the developing countries live should make us cry out for more responsibility in bringing life into this world!

About the Authors

DR. ANTHONY P. PEZZOTTA hails from Bergamo, Italy. He studied fifteen years in Roman Catholic seminaries of the Salesians of Don Bosco in Italy, England, Spain and Germany. He was ordained a Catholic priest on February 11, 1961 in Turin by His Eminence Cardinal Maurilio Fossati, then Archbishop of that diocese. In the Catholic Church, Dr. Pezzotta holds undergraduate degrees in Philosophy and Greek, and the equivalent to a master's degree in Theology from the Salesian Pontifical University in Rome. In the Philippines, he was made a director of schools and seminaries, as well as a rector of local Salesian communities (1964-1974).

On February 26, 1974, after studying the Scriptures on his own and through the testimony of Rev. Ernesto Montealegre, a Filipino Baptist pastor, Tony (as he likes to be called) trusted Christ alone as Savior and Lord of his life, left his church and joined the Santa Cruz Baptist Church, in which he was baptized on March 3, 1974. There he met Zita Vitangcol, a Sunday School teacher, whom he later married. God blessed them with three children: Marie, Angela, and Daniel.

Tony completed a Master's degree from Denver Seminary (Denver, Colorado) in 1975, and was given an honorary Doctor of Divinity degree from Western Seminary (Portland, Oregon) in 1991.

In 1975, after finishing their studies, Tony and Zita joined the First Baptist Church of West Los Angeles, U.S.A., where Tony